CIVIL WAR DELAWARE

Civil War Delaware

The First State Divided

Michael Morgan

Published by The History Press
Charleston, SC 29403
www.historypress.net

Front cover: Fort Delaware from *Harper's Weekly*, June 2, 1863.
Courtesy of the Delaware Public Arvhives.
Back cover: General Alfred T.A. Torbert. *Courtesy of the Deleware Public Archives.*

First published 2012

Manufactured in the United States

ISBN 978.1.60949.445.2

Library of Congress CIP data applied for.

Notice: The information in this book is true and complete to the best of our knowledge. It is offered without guarantee on the part of the author or The History Press. The author and The History Press disclaim all liability in connection with the use of this book.

Contents

Preface

Delaware, with an industrial north and an agricultural south, is an instructive prism through which to view the Civil War. Geographically positioned across vital Northern supply lines, Delaware, a slave state, sent proportionally more troops to fight for the Union than any free state. Torn by the political strife that mirrored the nation, Delaware supported President Lincoln's call to save the Union and rejected any plans for the emancipation of the state's slaves. By focusing on some of the heroes, soldiers and scoundrels, this work highlights Delaware's involvement in the Civil War.

An accurate portrait of Delaware in the Civil War would not be possible without the images from the Delaware Public Archives. I would like to thank Randy L. Goss, coordinator of accessioning and processing/photo archivist/preservation officer at the archives, for his efforts in securing most of the images in this book. I would also like to thank my son, Tom, for his technical assistance for all computer issues. Finally, I would like to thank my wife, Madelyn, for her constant editorial advice and support. She read every word in this book numerous times and spent countless hours correcting my spelling, punctuation and grammar. Without her help and support, this book would not have been possible.

Letters of Stephen T. Buckson of the Fourth Regiment Delaware Volunteers are part of the Civil War holdings of the Delaware Public Archives. *Courtesy of the Delaware Public Archives.*

Chapter 1

First State on the Fence

Delaware Enters the Debate

For a time our valleys will echo with the roar of artillery, and our mountains will ring with the reports of the rifle.
—Senator John Middleton Clayton

The end of this, we say is war—civil war," John Middleton Clayton of Delaware announced on March 4, 1830.[1] Tall, handsome and the youngest member of the United States Senate, Clayton declared that South Carolina was precipitating a crisis that would destroy the Union. The Delaware senator was born in 1796 in Dagsboro, a quiet hamlet on the banks of Pepper's Creek, a tributary of the Indian River, which, like most of the rivers in Delaware, was a lazy, slow-moving waterway akin to those found in the Carolina coastal plains.[2]

Running from north to south, Delaware has only three counties: New Castle, Kent and Sussex. Clayton was born in Sussex County, home to bitter political discord that stretched back to before the time of the American Revolution. Lewes, a salty maritime town near Cape Henlopen at the mouth of the Delaware Bay, had been the county seat during the colonial period. For years, Lewes dominated Sussex County's unruly politics, which pitted the coastal region against the more conservative inland areas. During the raucous election of 1787, the militia was called to restore order in the town and entered Lewes "with colors flying, and themselves furnished with pistols, clubs, cutlasses &c to the great terror of the peaceable inhabitants of

Senator John Middleton Clayton warned that sectional differences would lead to civil war. *Courtesy of the Delaware Public Archives.*

said town, and did then and there beat and wound several people."[3] In 1791, the people of the inland areas of Sussex County (where slavery was an entrenched institution) wrested control of the county government and moved the county seat from Lewes to Georgetown, a newly created town ten miles from Clayton's birthplace. Although small crossroad towns dotted the Delaware landscape, most people lived on farms where some of the houses were unbelievably small. Some contained fewer than four hundred square feet, smaller than a modern garage.[4] These tiny houses were built as simple rectangles or squares in which the first floor contained one or two multipurpose rooms. These areas were furnished with tables, chests, beds and other items that could be used for more than one function. Chests served as seats as well as storage containers; tables served as counters where meals could be prepared and eaten. At night, furniture could be shifted, and the floor became a common sleeping area. The homes were lit by fireplaces, candles and oil lamps; residents who had let their flames go out went to neighbors to borrow fire.

North of Sussex County lay Kent County, with more small farms, fewer slaves and containing Dover, the state capital. Geographically positioned in the middle of the state, Dover, the seat of Kent County, was a small, normally quiet town, except when it was swollen by the lawmakers, lawyers and lobbyists when the legislature was in session. With no port or deep-water facilities and little industry, Dover had little potential to be a big city. That claim would go to Wilmington.

On the northern reaches of New Castle County, Wilmington was separated from the rest of the state by the new Chesapeake and Delaware Canal that cut across New Castle County fifteen miles south of the city. In 1830, Wilmington

Small houses were not uncommon in rural Delaware. *Courtesy of the Delaware Public Archives.*

was emerging from the shadow of Philadelphia thirty miles to the north. The budding city was nestled between Brandywine Creek and the Christina River near where the two waterways merged and flowed into the Delaware River. The Christina was blessed with port facilities capable of accommodating oceangoing vessels. The swift-moving Brandywine provided power for grist, textile and paper mills and, most importantly, the Du Pont powder mills.

A pupil of the noted French chemist Antoine Lavoisier, Eleuthère Irénée du Pont de Nemours founded a high-quality gunpowder mill on Brandywine Creek in 1802.[5] Du Pont powder featured an eagle on the packaging, and the ornithologist and poet Alexander Wilson was moved to write:

> *From foaming Brandywine's rough shores it came,*
> *To sportsmen deer its merits and its name;*
> *Du Pont's best Eagle, matchless for its power,*
> *Strong, swift and fatal, as the bird it bore.*[6]

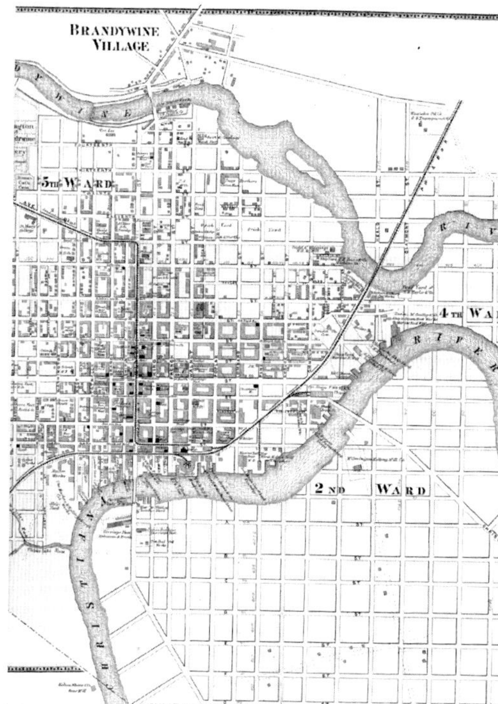

Left: Wilmington was nestled between the Brandywine Creek to the north (top) and the Christina River to the south (bottom). *Courtesy of the Delaware Public Archives.*

Below: Paper mills, as well as the Du Pont powder works, rested on the banks of Brandywine Creek. *Courtesy of the Delaware Public Archives.*

The Du Pont mills quickly developed into the premier gunpowder factory in the United States, and when the tariff debate erupted, most residents of Wilmington favored a high tariff to protect the city's growing industry. Overshadowed by Philadelphia, Wilmington was developing into a significant port town, and the du Pont mills made the town unique.

All three Delaware counties shared the state's deep devotion to the federal Union. Owned by the Penn family as a colony, Delaware had a long history of being the stepchild of other governments. First settled by the Dutch and the Swedes, Delaware had been harassed by Maryland until the colony was taken over by the English and acquired by William Penn to protect the maritime approaches to Pennsylvania. Known as the "Three Counties on the Delaware," the colony was the least of Penn's holdings, and the American Revolution had given Delaware independence from Pennsylvania as well as from Great Britain. When the federal Constitution was written, Delaware, the least populous state, saw an opportunity to protect itself from the domination of the larger states. Delaware was the first to ratify the Constitution and bore the nickname the "First State" proudly. In contrast, Rhode Island, smaller in area but larger in population, was the last of the original thirteen states to join the federal union.

As much of Delaware mirrored the country, so did the schooling of Senator Clayton. After attending the Lewes Academy in southern Delaware, Clayton went north to receive a rock-ribbed New England education at Yale. Following his graduation in 1815, Clayton returned to Delaware to practice law in Georgetown, where he quickly earned a reputation with his eloquent speech, well-mannered presentations and skilled questions.[7]

He was elected to the United States Senate in 1828, and two years later, a dispute over the sale of public lands exploded into a debate on the nature of the federal Union in a series of speeches by Robert Y. Hayne of South Carolina and Daniel Webster of Massachusetts. In a day when speeches lasted hours and touched on many topics, Hayne was strident in his defense of states' rights, the South Carolina doctrine of nullification and slavery. When it came to fugitive slaves and the abolitionists, Hayne minced no words:

> *Shedding weak tears over sufferings which had existence in their own sickly imaginations, these "friends of humanity" set themselves systematically to work to seduce the slaves of the south from their masters…And what has been the consequence? Go to these cities now and ask the question. Visit the dark and narrow lanes, and obscure recesses, which have been assigned by common consent as the abodes of those outcasts of the world, the free*

people of color. Sir, there does not exist, on the face of the whole earth, a population so poor, so wretched, so vile, so loathsome, so utterly destitute of all the comforts, conveniences, and decencies of life, as the unfortunate blacks of Philadelphia, and New York and Boston.[8]

When Webster answered Hayne, his eloquence soared to an end with a phrase that was repeated in Northern schoolhouses for a generation:

Let their last feeble and lingering glance rather behold the gorgeous ensign of the republic, now known and honored throughout the earth, still full high advanced, its arms and trophies streaming in their original luster, not a stripe erased or polluted, nor a single Star obscured, bearing for its motto, no such miserable interrogatory as "What is all this worth?" nor those other words of delusion and folly, "Liberty first and Union afterwards"; but everywhere, spread all over in characters of living light, blazing on all its ample folds, as they float over the sea and over the land, and in every wind under the whole heavens, that other sentiment, dear to every true American heart,—Liberty and Union, now and for ever, one and inseparable![9]

On March 4, 1830, Clayton rose to speak. The young Delaware senator attacked the heart of the South Carolina nullification doctrine:

For he [Hayne] *informed us that a State Convention might be called, and that might nullify the oppressive law—after which, he thought Congress must acquiesce by abandoning the power. The amount of this is, that one State is to govern all the rest whenever she may choose to declare, by Convention, that a law is unconstitutional.*[10]

At the end of the lengthy speech, Clayton described the horrors of the war to come:

For a time our valleys will echo with the roar of artillery, and our mountains will ring with the reports of the rifle. The storm of civil war will howl fearfully through the land, from the Atlantic border to the wildest recesses of the West, covering with desolation every field which has been crowned with verdure by the culture of freemen, and now resounding with the echoes of our happiness and industry. But the tempest must subside, and be succeeded by the deep calm and sullen gloom of despotism:—after which, the voice of a freeman shall never again be heard within our

> *borders, unless in the fearful and suppressed whispers of the traveler from some distant land who shall visit the scene of our destruction to gaze in sorrow on the melancholy ruin.*[11]

Along with the texts of speeches of Hayne and Webster, Clayton's address was one of the most widely circulated of the debate.[12] Despite the inflammatory words, the nullification crisis passed without violence. Clayton's speech, however, marked him as a rising star on the political scene. The questions of nullification, secession and slavery continued to simmer, and three decades later, America was still haunted by Clayton's 1830 prediction that "the end of this, we say is war—civil war."

Nat Turner Frightens Delaware

Delaware has yet the mark of the beast upon her.
—*William Yates*

The nullification crisis was still boiling when Nat Turner led a slave rebellion in Virginia that resulted in the death of nearly five dozen white people. After Turner's bloody rampage, rumors spread that bands of runaway slaves were gathering in the Great Cypress Swamp on the border between Delaware and Maryland. On election day, rumors were rife that a slave uprising had been planned when a band of armed men was spotted near the Nanticoke River near Seaford. The men were divided into two parties, and one group appeared to open fire on the others, some of whom fell to the ground as if they had been shot. Immediately, some frightened observers ran into Seaford and reported that armed bands of blacks had landed south of Seaford. The marauders reportedly killed several white men and were preparing to march through southern Delaware.

It was all a hoax! For reasons only known to the participants, the shooting had been staged, and no one had been shot.[13] The prank ignited a firestorm of fear. Several years after the event, the *Delaware Register* reported, "The fearful ran and hid themselves in the woods, while the stout hearted flew to arms."[14] A messenger was immediately dispatched to warn those who were attending the election to return home at once to protect their families. Having thoroughly alarmed the white population of western Sussex County, the report of the supposed uprising was carried quickly to Kent County, where the rumor expanded to include 1,500 armed African Americans from

Maryland who had landed on the banks of the Nanticoke River and were marching northward.

The purported slave rebellion failed to materialize and the threat of an uprising was proven to be groundless, but this failed to calm the hearts of many people in Sussex and Kent Counties. Town meetings were held, and resolutions were passed to disarm all African Americans, free or slave. Those men capable of bearing arms were organized into squads of six or seven to patrol the streets at night. As the *Delaware Register* commented, "Preparations for war were made on a more extensive scale than would have been done, had it been reduced to a certainty, that a foreign enemy had landed an army at Lewes."[15]

When the Delaware state legislature met in January, a bill passed that made it illegal for free African Americans to own firearms or hold religious meetings. Many whites believed that the black churches were fomenting rebellion and deemed that religious services could only be held under the supervision of "respectable white persons." In addition, out-of-state African American preachers, who were suspected of bringing plans of insurrection to Delaware, were banned. Violators were subject to be sold as slaves. As the *Delaware Register* commented, "It was a most superb farce and so considered by a large majority of the people."[16] Some provisions of this Draconian measure went unenforced, and the law became a monument to a hoax.

The only known photograph of a Delaware slave. *Courtesy of the Delaware Public Archives.*

A half dozen years after Nat Turner's rebellion spread fears of a slave uprising through Delaware, William Yates (an agent for the American Anti-Slavery Society) arrived in Delaware "to learn from personal observations the condition of the free people of color within its borders; and to ascertain the sentiments which prevail in regard to the remnant of slavery still existing there."[17] Yates found that the laws passed after Nat Turner's rebellion contained "some noble and just provisions, but its general scope and design seem rather to have been to degrade, to crush, and to render [African Americans] powerless."[18] In addition, Delaware law made it illegal to sell slaves to out-of-state buyers, but Yates discovered, "I have learned the appalling fact, that in spite of the penalty, the infamous business of selling slaves out of the State has been carried on to an alarming extent."[19]

On the whole, however, Yates was optimistic that slavery in Delaware was on its last legs. He argued that the nine hundred slave owners would be overwhelmed by the fifty-three thousand white residents who did not own slaves. Yates predicted, "Delaware must be the entering wedge in the great work of emancipation in our country…Delaware is a most critical ground in the contest waging between liberty and slavery, between light and darkness."[20] Economic and social pressures, however, did not cause slavery in Delaware to wither away. The institution remained entrenched in Sussex County until the end of the Civil War, and during that time, as William Yates put it, "Delaware has yet the mark of the beast upon her."[21]

The Lone Star of Illinois

It was a war of conquest brought into existence to catch votes.
—Abraham Lincoln

When Abraham Lincoln arrived in Wilmington, Delaware, in 1848, the town was booming. Fed by an influx of Irish immigrants who found employment in the town's carriage works, tanneries and shipyards, Wilmington's population had increased 50 percent in the 1840s and contained upward of thirteen thousand residents.[22] Although this was paltry by national standards—the population of Greater Philadelphia was around a half million—Wilmington was far and away the only Delaware community to justify the term "city." Despite a few hundred slaves who lived within the town limits, Wilmington was a decidedly Northern city whose growth was unique in Delaware.

In 1848, Lincoln was in Philadelphia attending the national Whig convention that nominated General Zachary Taylor, the hero of the Battle of Buena Vista, as its presidential candidate. Delaware was a Whig state led by the state's most important politician, Senator John M. Clayton, whose

This postwar image shows early nineteenth-century houses with peaked roofs in Wilmington. *Courtesy of the Delaware Public Archives.*

elegant speech envisaging the horrors of civil war was now an echo from the distant past. At the convention, Clayton was Delaware's favorite son candidate for the presidency, but he recognized that he did not have enough support to garner the nomination, and the Delaware politician threw his support to Taylor.[23]

After the Philadelphia convention, the Whigs and their Democratic rivals organized competing ratification conventions in Wilmington to kick off the presidential campaign. The Democrats met in the afternoon, and later that evening, the Whigs held their rally at the new Fourth Street Market House that, as a mark of Wilmington's growing prosperity, had been built to replace an earlier building that had served the city for over a century. The Greek Revival building was festooned with flags and banners as supporters of the Whigs crowded into Fourth and Market Streets to the patriotic tunes of an enthusiastic band. When Lincoln, the clean-shaven, chiseled-face rail-splitter, stepped onto the balcony of the Market House, he was introduced as the "Lone Star of Illinois," and the throng responded with three cheers.[24]

In the years since Clayton had warned that the United States was on a course for civil war, the sectional divide had been temporarily mended. Under the firm hand of Andrew Jackson, compromises had been grudgingly patched together, and the sale of public lands and the tariff no longer inflamed talk of nullification. There had been no compromise on slavery; thus, the peculiar institution festered like a blister that would not heal. With the stunning defeat of Mexico in a war enthusiastically supported by the Southern states, the extension of slavery to the Pacific Ocean appeared possible. But when Lincoln began to speak on the Market House balcony, the Lone Star of Illinois lambasted the Polk administration for its highhanded use of the veto and the manner in which it carried on the war. He referred to the abuse of power in James K. Polk's administration and what Lincoln considered the utter disregard of the will of the people.[25] As for slavery, Lincoln stated that he did not think that the war with Mexico was begun for the purpose of extending slave territory but was "a war of conquest brought into existence to catch votes."[26]

Lincoln's Wilmington speech was well received, and the next morning, he boarded a train for Washington to finish his term as a congressman. The Whig candidate, Zachary Taylor, was victorious in the election of 1848, and he appointed Senator Clayton secretary of state. The Dagsboro native negotiated the Clayton-Bulwer Treaty with Great Britain that helped clear the way for the construction of the Panama Canal. The question of slavery, however, continued to fester.[27]

The Escape of Theophilus Collins

A nigger and a mule hadn't any feeling.
—David Houston, Sussex County slave owner

When the slave Theophilus Collins saw David Houston draw his knife, Collins knew that he was in a fight for his life. By all accounts, Houston was a brutal man. Living near Lewes in the years before the Civil War, Houston used little restraint when disciplining his slaves. According to one of Houston's slaves, "If you didn't do the work right, he got contrary, and wouldn't give you anything to eat for a whole day at a time." Houston once said, "A nigger and a mule hadn't any feeling."[28] Once, when a slave was sick, Houston beat him so badly with a chunk of wood that the slave died.

Theophilus Collins was well aware of the way his master treated slaves when Houston confronted him in his dining room. Collins recalled:

> *I was in servitude under a man named Houston, near Lewes, Delaware; he was a very mean man, he didn't allow you enough to eat, nor enough*

> *clothes to wear. He never allowed a drop of tea, or coffee or sugar, and if you didn't eat your breakfast before day*[break] *he wouldn't allow you any, but would drive you out without any. He had a wife; she was mean, too, meaner than he was.*[29]

That night Collins had gone to church, and Houston was furious. Many white owners believed that sermons about Moses and the deliverance of the Hebrews out of Egypt encouraged slaves to flee to the North. Houston had already lost several slaves to the Underground Railroad, and he was determined that Collins would not escape and would pay for going to church. Houston called Collins into the dining room, locked all the doors and ordered, "Pull off your shirt." When Collins defiantly replied, "No sir, I won't," Houston got a cowhide whip and, using the hard butt, gave the African American twenty blows on his head. Houston again demanded that Collins take off his shirt, and when he refused, the slave master tore it off. Houston ordered Collins to cross his hands, and when he refused, the infuriated Houston grabbed a gun and hit the slave so hard that he broke the weapon's breech. He then seized fire tongs and beat Collins over the head. Next, the enraged Houston took a fireplace shovel and began to beat the slave until the handle broke; then he took the shovel blade and hit Collins in the head with it. Beaten, bleeding and fearing for his life, Collins attempted to break out of the locked room, but when he made a move toward the door, Houston picked up a pocketknife and sliced Collins "as hard as he could rip across my stomach; right away he began stabbing me about the head."[30]

Despite his wounds, Collins was able to get past Houston and break out of the room. Using his hands to keep the wound in his stomach closed, Collins made his way to Georgetown, where three sympathetic doctors treated him. When he had recovered sufficiently enough to travel, Collins joined several other fugitive slaves and headed northward. Following the Underground Railroad, Collins and his party made their way through Milford, Dover, Middletown and Wilmington. From there, they traveled to Philadelphia and freedom.

By the 1850s, the Underground Railroad had developed several routes through Delaware. In the northern part of the state, the Maryland border was about fifteen miles from downtown Wilmington, where the city's free black and friendly white residents were ready to help the fugitives to reach Philadelphia. A number of escaped slaves also used the Delaware River to reach free states.[31] In addition, there were several routes on the Underground Railroad that ran the length of the state. None knew these clandestine trails better than Harriet Tubman. Born a slave in 1820, she worked as a field hand and house servant across the Maryland border in Dorchester County. In 1844, she married John Tubman, a free black. Five years later, Harriet learned that she was about to be sold down the river to the Deep South, where the life of a slave was often torturous, exhausting and short-lived. On the other hand, slaves who ran away from masters were often hunted, recaptured and brutally punished. After Nat Turner's bloody rebellion in 1831, slave states passed laws that made it illegal to teach slaves

This map shows Delaware's proximity to Philadelphia to the north, Baltimore and Washington to the west. The dark line running north to south indicates the Delaware Railroad. *Courtesy of the Delaware Public Archives.*

to read and write. Unable to read signposts, runaway slaves had to rely on directions from strangers, who often betrayed runaway slaves to collect rewards offered by the fugitives' masters. Despite the risk, Tubman decided that she would have either liberty or death, and in 1849, she slipped away from her master's plantation.

When she began her flight for freedom, Tubman followed the Choptank River, which flowed out of central Delaware southward through Maryland. During the day, Tubman traveled upstream toward Delaware, where friendly abolitionists could guide her toward Pennsylvania and freedom. At night, she searched the sky for stars of the "drinking gourd," which pointed to the North Star that served as a steady guidepost on the road out of slavery.

Harriet Tubman was able to avoid the slave catchers. She successfully made her way through Delaware to Philadelphia, where she joined others who had escaped slavery. Unlike most of the fugitives who had risked their lives to gain their freedom, Tubman made a decision that would earn her the title "Moses." At the risk of recapture and death, she decided to return to Maryland to lead other slaves across Delaware to freedom. Tubman made use of safe houses at Seaford, Laurel, Concord, Georgetown, Millsboro, Lewes, Milford, Blackbird, Frederica, Smyrna, Delaware City, Middletown, New Castle, Dover, Camden and Wilmington,[32] where she sometimes stopped at the house of Thomas Garrett on Shipley Street. From his Wilmington home, Garrett assisted hundreds of slaves on their way to Pennsylvania and freedom. Although his house was under almost constant surveillance and a reward of $10,000 was offered for his capture, Garrett was able to thwart all legal attempts to stop his activities for nearly three decades. In 1848, he was prosecuted and convicted in a suit brought by slave owners. According to tradition, when the judge announced the large fine that was to be levied against him and suggested that Garrett refrain from breaking the law in the future, the Quaker resolutely commented, "Judge, thou has not left me a dollar, but I say to thee, and to all in this courtroom, that if any knows of a fugitive who wants shelter and a friend, send him to Thomas Garrett and he will befriend him."[33] Harriet Beecher Stowe said that the character Simeon Halliday in *Uncle Tom's Cabin*, a Quaker who risked fine and imprisonment to help fugitive slaves, was inspired by Thomas Garrett.[34] By his own account, Garrett assisted 2,700 fugitives, the vast majority of whom were fleeing masters from outside Delaware to freedom.[35]

Election Night in Wilmington

Republican demonstrations are far more brilliant & imposing than others.
—Anna M. Ferris

"Tonight we had one of the great political demonstrations that have been the distinguishing feature of this campaign," Anna M. Ferris noted in her diary. As the daughter of Wilmington watchmaker and local historian Benjamin Ferris, she inherited her Quaker father's proclivity for sensing historical significance, and when she watched the parade before the 1860 presidential election, she was duly impressed by "a great torch light procession with 400 Equestrians followed by a countless multitude on foot, with brilliant fire works & transparencies."[36]

There was an excitement in the air as the torchlight parade wound its way through the streets of Wilmington, a town that had grown to over twenty thousand residents. Home of the state's best private schools and Delaware's only college, Wilmington had a vibrant cultural life where citizens enjoyed theatrical productions, concerts and lectures. The city's mills and factories turned out cotton goods, flour, carriages, morocco leather and ships. At a time when no other Delaware community could claim to be a center of heavy industry, Wilmington specialized in the production of railroad cars and other vehicles, earning it the nickname "Queen of the Carriage Builders."[37]

As Wilmington thrived, the Du Pont mills thrived as well. Lining the banks of the Brandywine, the company's buildings were three-quarters solid stone, with the side fronting the river constructed of flimsy wood so that an explosion would funnel the blast over the Brandywine. This resulted in the unfortunate expression "crossing the river" to describe workers who had died in explosions. In 1857, Alexis I. du Pont, one of the sons of the company's founder, was in one of the buildings when a fire started. Oblivious to the danger, du Pont attempted to put out the fire with his hands but failed. The flames ignited some of the sweepings, and the resulting explosion blew du Pont away from the building. With a courage common to the du Ponts and with his clothing afire, he raced into the burning mill to extinguish the flames and prevent an additional explosion. Again, he failed. A blast ripped through the building, and du Pont was fatally injured. One of his last acts was to direct his son, Eugene, to use his suspenders to tie a tourniquet around his legs to stop the bleeding. In addition to du Pont, five other men were killed in the explosion.[38] Periodic accidental explosions did not deter the company. In 1860, the Du Pont mills were the largest producer of gunpowder in the

A modern view of the stone buildings at the Du Pont powder mills built with one wooden side so that an explosion would direct the force of the blast across the river. *Photo by Michael Morgan.*

United States.[39] The company was led by Henry du Pont, one of the sons of the firm's founder and a dedicated Union man.

When Anna Ferris watched the political demonstrations in 1860, the Whigs were nowhere to be found. In the 1850s, John Clayton's old party had been shipwrecked on the reef of slavery. For a time, many former Whigs coalesced around the Know-Nothing standard and captured the governor's office and many seats in the state legislature, but that temporary coalition foundered when the Know-Nothings pushed through a law banning alcohol. By the 1860s, a People's Party had emerged, and the embryonic Republican Party competed for the former Whig voters.[40]

The foundering of the Whigs left Delaware open for the Democrats to dominate the state, which voted Democratic in the 1852 and 1856 presidential elections. The eminent Delaware historian Harold Hancock wrote, "The backbone of the party was the farmers of Kent and Sussex counties, who had some of the same problems and interest as the southern Democrats. Even though many did not own slaves, they were particularly sensitive to what they referred to as the 'nigger' questions and the status of the free Negro."[41]

In Delaware, however, the Democrats were divided between a faction led by aristocratic Senator James A. Bayard, whose family included two former senators, and a faction headed by Senator Willard Saulsbury, whose brothers, Gove and Eli, were also powers in Delaware politics. Willard was a hard-drinking, hardnosed politician whose "Party of the three brothers" wrestled with Bayard for control of the state Democratic organization.

In April 1860, Bayard and Willard Saulsbury arrived in Charleston, South Carolina to attend the Democratic Party's nominating convention. It did not take long for the fireworks to ignite. Bayard and his ally, Representative William G. Whiteley, were supporters of the Southern Democrats. The Saulsburys were supporters of Stephen Douglas, the favorite of the Northern Democrats. In Charleston, the Democrats were unable to agree on a candidate who satisfied both wings of the party, and the Southern Democrats left the meeting hall and organized a splinter group that elected Bayard its permanent chairman.

Gove Saulsbury, one of the three Saulsbury brothers. *Courtesy of the Delaware Public Archives.*

Both factions adjourned without nominating a presidential candidate, and they agreed to meet separately in Baltimore. When Whiteley appeared before the committee on credentials for the Southern Democrats, he was confronted by Sam Townsend, a cantankerous Delaware railroad man, peach planter, canner and outspoken politician. Angry words were exchanged between the two men, and the words led to an exchange of blows. The two were separated, and a certain amount of decorum was restored. But the next morning, Whiteley showed up at Townsend's hotel, and the fight was resumed. Townsend gave Whiteley a sound drubbing and knocked him to the floor. When Whiteley got up, a pistol fell out of his coat, but Townsend retrieved it and kept it until police arrived. Townsend won the fight but lost the battle over his admission to the convention; the credentials committee seated Whiteley.[42] The Southern Democrats went on to nominate John Breckinridge, and the Northerners selected Douglas as their standard-bearer. The Republicans nominated Lincoln to be their candidate. A group that feared the country was headed toward civil war quickly organized into the Constitutional Union Party, nominating John Bell as their candidate.

In the four-way race, each candidate had some support in Delaware, where elections were celebrated with great pomp and ceremony. In Sussex County, voters gathered in the county seat at Georgetown to hear the election results. On Return Day, as the occasion was called, booths were set up in the public square to serve cakes and candies in addition to more substantial food, such as fish, oysters, rabbit meat and opossum. Some voters dressed in outlandish costumes that added more zest to the celebration. The candidates

The Georgetown Brick Hotel was across the public square from the courthouse where the voting took place. *Courtesy of the Delaware Public Archives.*

were met by admiring crowds, and when the results were announced from the courthouse window, the winners were hoisted onto men's shoulders and paraded around the public circle.[43]

As election day 1860 neared, Anna Ferris observed in Wilmington, "Republican demonstrations are far more brilliant & imposing than others… This outside show & enthusiasm is a more potent stimulant to human nature than reason or principle & carries the masses with it."[44]

When the votes were counted, Breckinridge and the Southern Democrats carried the state, with Bell, the Constitutional Union Party nominee, second. The Republican, Lincoln, finished third. Douglas was a distant last. The split in the Democratic Party enabled the Republican's George P. Fisher, who had been a private secretary to Senator Clayton, to win the state's lone congressional seat.[45] When the election returns indicated that Lincoln had a majority of the electoral votes, South Carolina and other slaveholding states immediately prepared for secession, ignoring John Middleton Clayton's haunting words: "The storm of civil war will howl fearfully through the land, from the Atlantic border to the wildest recesses of the West, covering with desolation every field."[46]

Chapter 2

Delaware Decides

Southern Overture

The people will demand a convention and Delaware will co-operate with Mississippi.
—Henry Dickinson

When Abraham Lincoln won the four-way presidential election in November 1860, he garnered less than 40 percent of the popular vote; but except for New Jersey, the Lone Star of Illinois swept the non-slaveholding states to win a resounding victory in the Electoral College.[47] In December 1860, South Carolina declared:

> *A geographical line has been drawn across the Union, and all the States north of that line have united in the election of a man to the high office of President of the United States, whose opinions and purposes are hostile to slavery. He is to be entrusted with the administration of the common Government, because he has declared that that "Government cannot endure permanently half slave, half free," and that the public mind must rest in the belief that slavery is in the course of ultimate extinction.*[48]

With that statement, South Carolina withdrew from the Union.

Not only did other slaveholding states prepare to secede from the Union, but several of the Southern states also sent emissaries to Delaware to entice the First State to join them. During the first week of January, David Clopton,

William Burton was governor when the state rejected the Confederacy's overtures. *Courtesy of the Delaware Public Archives.*

appointed by the governor of Alabama, arrived in Dover, where the state legislature was meeting, to confer with Governor William Burton, a Democrat who blamed the crisis on the abolitionists and the efforts of Northern states to block the enforcement of the Fugitive Slave Law. In his written message to Burton, Clopton shrewdly argued that the incoming Lincoln administration was determined to prevent any more slave states from entering the Union, to enact laws to prevent the capture of fugitive slaves and to foment slave insurrections by disseminating abolitionist materials. In short, Clopton maintained of the Lincoln administration, "Its animus… is hostility to the institution of slavery as it exists in the Southern States."[49] Governor Burton accepted Clopton's message without comment, but the Alabama emissary believed that "a large majority of the people of Delaware will defend the South."

The same week that Clopton was attempting to meet with Governor Burton, Henry Dickinson addressed a joint session of the state legislature. In his speech (which was met with a mixture of applause and hisses), Dickinson forcibly asserted the right of South Carolina to secede and invited Delaware to join the nascent Southern confederacy. Dickinson then declared that if South Carolina was not allowed to leave the Union, war was inevitable.[50]

In response to the Southern overture, the Delaware legislature passed a resolution condemning secession, but Dickinson remained convinced that support for the South was strong. He wired the governor of Mississippi, "The Governor, officers of State, and six-sevenths of the people of Delaware are cordially with Mississippi in the Southern cause. The present Legislature opposed to immediate secession. The people will demand a convention and Delaware will co-operate with Mississippi."[51]

Six weeks later, when D.C. Campbell, an emissary from Georgia, arrived in Dover, seven states had formed the Confederate States of America, and preparations were being made for the inauguration of Jefferson Davis. Campbell had learned that the Delaware legislature was likely to be unsympathetic to secession, and he decided not to meet with the legislature, instead confining his lobbying efforts to Governor Burton. Campbell, like the emissaries from Alabama and Mississippi, sought to explain why his state had seceded and why Delaware should join the Confederacy. In a message to Governor Burton, Campbell said, "[Georgia] has now passed the Rubicon and with no intention of taking any steps backward." Campbell went on to argue that Delaware, in proportion to its population, may not have had as deep-seated an interest in slavery as the other border states, yet he believed that Delaware sympathized with Georgia in interest, sentiment and principle. Campbell believed that the force of events would soon throw Delaware's lot in with the Confederacy.[52]

Unlike the other emissaries, whose arguments revolved around slavery, Campbell took a different tack. Recognizing the growth of Wilmington, he maintained, "Those Southern border States, therefore, who are far advanced in manufacturing and mechanical skill have now tendered to them the entire South for a market and that without a rival."[53] In closing, Campbell made a final plea for Delaware to join a confederacy of all of the slaveholding states so that it could add "her full quota of talent and moral worth and contributing her full quota to its prosperity."[54]

When Campbell left Delaware, he, like the other two emissaries, was convinced that Delaware's principal interests were with the South and the state would not maintain its ties with the North. He argued that whenever Virginia and Maryland withdrew from the Union, Delaware would follow in their footsteps.[55] Campbell was wrong. As February turned into March and Abraham Lincoln was inaugurated as president, the First State remained steadfastly in the Union.

All for the Union

The sentries were firing at will and yelling like demons.
—William Seville

"The ball has been opened at last and war is inaugurated," the *Delaware State Journal and Statesman* reported on April 16, 1861. The Wilmington newspaper went on to report, "The batteries on Sullivan's Island, Morris Island and other points, opened on Fort Sumter at 4 o'clock this morning [April 12]."[56]

When the Confederate guns fired on Fort Sumter, the Southern overtures to Delaware ended. But there a remained a significant number of Southern sympathizers in the state, and they made up the bulk of some militia companies.[57] Governor Burton appointed Henry du Pont, head of the powder company, major general of militia, with authority over these military companies.[58] Born in 1812 and a graduate of West Point, du Pont had taken over the direction of the powder mills after his brother, Alexis, died in the 1857 explosion.[59] Du Pont was a firm Union man, and he acted quickly to assign loyal militia that included many powder millworkers to guard the works along the Brandywine.[60] In addition, du Pont moved to disarm those militia groups that sympathized with the South.[61]

The same issue of the *Delaware State Journal and Statesman* that reported the firing on Fort Sumter also advertised President Lincoln's call for seventy-five thousand volunteers, and Union men began to enlist in the First Regiment, Delaware Volunteers. Adjutant William P. Seville, who was the regimental historian, wrote that the warnings of a disastrous war were all political posturing,

> *but when State after State adopted ordinances of secession; when armed bodies were organized and drilled; when the note of hostile preparation rose on every hand in the rebellious States; and, finally, when a furious force set itself in battle array before Fort Sumter, and the dreadful overture to civil war was begun on the morning of Friday, April 12, 1861, by the opening of the rebel guns on that work and the revered national flag, all doubts were instantly dissipated.*[62]

During the 1860 presidential race, all four candidates had significant support in Delaware, and political leaders worked to enlist every man to their cause by forming clubs, such as the Wide Awakes, Bell Men and Minute Men. As was the case in many fraternal organizations, many of these political clubs sported distinctive uniforms and exercised in close-order drill that gave their parades military precision. Members of some of the Wilmington political clubs formed the nucleus of the first companies of recruits of the First Regiment of Delaware Volunteers.[63]

Initially, Companies A and B of the First Regiment drilled at the Institute Building on Market Street, which served as an armory and quarters for the troops. After two weeks, the regiment moved to the fairgrounds in the suburbs of the Wilmington, naming it Camp Brandywine. After a month of drilling, officers were elected: Henry H. Lockwood, a professor of mathematics and instructor of infantry tactics at the United States Naval Academy at Annapolis, Maryland, as colonel and John W. Andrews as lieutenant colonel.[64]

These three men joined the fight to preserve the Union. *Courtesy of the Delaware Public Archives.*

The ranks of the First Delaware Regiment filled quickly, but they lacked weapons and other military equipment. In addition, some suspected that Governor Burton, a Democrat, was in league with the Southern sympathizers. On April 19, 1861, Henry du Pont wrote to the secretary of war, Simon Cameron: "Volunteers are enrolling at Wilmington, several companies, but have no arms or equipments of any kind, all the arms, &c., belonging to the State being in the hands of the Governor's friends and not in the possession of Union men."[65]

In addition, du Pont was concerned about the safety of the powder works:

> *I will remark that the gunpowder mills in this neighborhood, of which I am at the head, are of importance to the Government in these times, from their extent and immense facilities of production. They are wholly unprotected, and there is not a musket or rifle in the place; but we have over 300 good men, true and loyal, and if we could get some 200 or 300 stand of arms from Frankford Arsenal and accoutrements, if there, we could take care of ourselves for the present, as far as mobs and disaffected persons are concerned.*[66]

Delaware men were flocking to the Union cause, and on Sunday, May 26, the regiment made its full dress parade as it marched through Wilmington before an immense crowd that lined the parade route.[67] Although the First

Staters looked like soldiers when they marched through the city, the Delaware troops still lacked soldierly discipline. The next week, the First Delaware was dispatched to Maryland to guard the railroad lines north of Baltimore. On the first night in camp, a deafening uproar arose that brought every man out of bed in an instant. "The sentries were firing at will and yelling like demons, while the men were tumbling out of the barracks in the direst confusion."[68] As the men streamed out of the building, they found the officers quietly directing the men to fall in. As the ranks were being formed, the racket among the sentinels settled down. The officers then lectured the men that they should bear in mind that no matter how vigorously the sentinels called, it was the sergeant of the guard who should respond and not the entire regiment.[69] In the coming years, the Delaware troops would become better disciplined and better soldiers. But for the moment, the war that the *Delaware State Journal and Statesman* had compared to a grand ball was a lark.

Some for the South

The arms that Delaware owns are in the hands of the secessionists.
—Charles du Pont Bird

"With a man or two from you to give directions and a hint that arms and men would come if necessary, the people of Sussex themselves would destroy the Delaware railroad terminating at Seaford, on the Nanticoke," Charles du Pont Bird wrote on April 26, 1861, in a message that was forwarded to General Robert E. Lee, the newly appointed commander of the Virginia military and naval forces. In his note, Bird offered his unsolicited opinion on the sentiment of the people of southern Delaware.[70] A week earlier, Federal troops moving through Baltimore, Maryland, had sparked a riot, and in the aftermath of the violence, the railroad bridges linking Philadelphia with Washington, D.C., were burned.

In the early seventeenth century, when Delaware was first settled, some of the European colonists arrived by way of the Nanticoke River. During colonial times, this convenient waterway allowed sailing vessels from the Chesapeake Bay to travel deep into the heart of southern Delaware. The river carried produce from Sussex County farms to Baltimore, Norfolk and other Chesapeake ports. During the first half of the nineteenth century, steamboats operating on the Nanticoke River linked residents from Seaford, Laurel and other southern Delaware communities with the rest of the world.

In 1856, the Delaware Railroad was completed to Seaford on the Nanticoke River, and it provided a quick link to Philadelphia, New York and the North. At the same time, the Nanticoke River continued to provide a convenient highway to the South. In his advice to Lee, Bird pointed out that the train line to Seaford offered an alternative route to ship troops and war materiel to the beleaguered nation's capital. Bird believed that the Federal government would take steps to secure this route, which would provide an alternate route to transport troops from the North by way of the Nanticoke River to the Chesapeake and then to Washington by the Potomac River. Bird advised, "A vessel or two sunk in the Nanticoke will hinder this design." In addition, there were a number of railroad trestles near Dover that could be destroyed easily.[71]

Although there was considerable sentiment in Delaware in favor of the Union, Bird believed that

> *the arms that Delaware owns are in the hands of the secessionists. The powder mills on the Brandywine (owned by relations of mine) should be secured at all hazards. With not a very large force, if we cannot hold them, they should be destroyed. Some of the du Ponts are friendly to the South. If it is possible to guard these works for a few weeks, the stock of powder for the Southern Confederacy would be largely increased.*

Bird implored Lee to act at once to "stop the hordes of the North."[72]

There is no record of Lee's having responded to Bird's letter, and the railroad through southern Delaware remained firmly in Federal control. Southern sympathizers, however, realized that there was another route to ship war materiel to the Confederate forces. To circumvent the Union control of the railroad, Rebel sympathizers shipped goods from New York City by sea to the Delaware coast and through the Indian River Inlet, where they could be carried overland through Sussex County to the Nanticoke River. So many Confederate agents were observed buying war materiel in New York that in August 1861, Hiram Barney, customs collector for New York City, wrote an urgent letter to Gideon Welles, the Union secretary of the navy, that he could not cite specific examples but general reports and numerous suspicious circumstances convinced him that "it is a matter of notoriety that articles of all kinds are constantly transmitted by way of Delaware and Maryland into eastern Virginia." Vessels, loaded with provisions and general stores, sailed from New York City, down the New Jersey coast and across the mouth of the Delaware

Well into the twentieth century, much of the Delaware coast was wild dunes, marshes and narrow inlets. *Courtesy of the Delaware Public Archives.*

Bay to inlets on the Delaware and Maryland coasts. Retracing a trade route that originated during colonial times, these vessels sailed across the coastal bays to the mainland, where they unloaded their war materiels and shipped them overland into Rebel hands. In his letter to Secretary Welles, Barney complained, "Our coasters are leaving daily for the Delaware and Maryland ports, loaded with general merchandise designed undoubtedly for the use of parties on the Virginia side."[73]

The New York customs collector believed that any attempt to require captains to file affidavits as to their destination would be circumvented by the Southern sympathizers. Barney thought that using small armed vessels that could negotiate the shallow water of the coastal inlets would be the best way to stop the clandestine trade with the South. He advised the secretary of the navy: "A few light-draft vessels, to run into the inlets and watch the coast from the Delaware Bay to the South, would be of great service."[74]

In addition to shipping war materiel to the South, a number of important residents of Sussex County slipped away to join the Confederate forces. There were enough Southern sympathizers from other slave states who remained loyal to organize regiments that served in the Confederate army, but there were not enough Delaware men who were willing to fight for the

Washington A. Vickers of Seaford, who joined the Confederate forces. *Courtesy of Delaware State Parks.*

South to form a distinct unit. Consequently, the records of those individuals who served in Southern forces—such as Washington Vickers of Seaford, who joined the Second Maryland Infantry, Confederate States of America—are scattered, and an exact tabulation cannot be made.[75]

The Most Humane Way to End the War

When the people of Delaware desire to abolish slavery within her borders, they will do so in their own way.
—Delaware General Assembly

In the late seventeenth century, William Burton was living on the Eastern Shore of Virginia when he decided to look for a new place to settle. As he sailed northward along the Delmarva coast, he ignored the smaller inlets that cut through the barrier islands in Virginia and Maryland. After he rounded the false cape at Fenwick Island, the intrepid colonist continued northward along the Delaware coast until he reached the Indian River Inlet. Turning westward, Burton navigated through the inlet until he spotted the high ground of Long Neck and, according to tradition, proclaimed, "I will look no more."[76]

During the next two centuries, the Burton family tree developed many branches, both black and white. In 1837, Noah Burton, an illiterate free African American handyman, sued one of his employers for nonpayment of wages. Burton presented as evidence a notched tally stick on which he recorded his work and wages and won his case, setting a precedent on the use of unconventional records.[77] At the start of the Civil War, William Burton was governor of Delaware, and a distant relative, Benjamin Burton, who owned twenty-eight slaves, was the largest slave owner in the state. Several months after the war started, the slaveholding Benjamin Burton received a request to meet with President Lincoln.

In July 1861, the Battle of Bull Run demonstrated that the Civil War would be a long, hard struggle that would cost millions of dollars and thousands of lives, and Lincoln was searching for a way to shorten the war. Several weeks after the battle, Benjamin Burton went to the White House, and when he was ushered into President Abraham Lincoln's office, he was greeted by the president and Congressman George P. Fisher.

Benjamin Burton promoted President Lincoln's plan of compensated emancipation. *Courtesy of the Delaware Public Archives.*

The Fisher family never lacked for courage. One of the congressman's ancestors was Bishop John Fisher, who was beheaded for opposing Henry VIII's divorce from Catherine of Aragon. Thomas Fisher, the congressman's father, held several important public offices in Sussex County. He commanded a brigade of Sussex County militia when the British bombarded Lewes during the War of 1812. Congressman Fisher inherited a robust physique from his father. He was over six feet tall with a military, straight-as-an-arrow bearing. Genial, affable and courteous, Fisher usually dressed in a blue cut-away coat with brass buttons and a ruffled shirt. After attending Dickinson College, Fisher studied law under John Clayton, and when Clayton became secretary of state, Fisher served as his confidential clerk. A rising star in Delaware politics, the Republican Fisher had run counter to the Democratic tide in 1860 to be elected to Delaware's seat in the House of Representatives.[78]

Although Lincoln declared that the war was being fought to preserve the Union, the president believed that a solution to the slavery question was the key to ending the rebellion. In late 1861, Lincoln devised a plan to end slavery, stop the war and save thousands of lives. The president first broached

Representative George Fisher risked his political career supporting Lincoln's compensated emancipation plan. *Courtesy of the Delaware Public Archives.*

the plan to Congressman Fisher, who suggested that Burton be brought to Washington to hear what Lincoln had in mind. Under Lincoln's plan, the Federal government would reimburse slave owners for their economic loss when they set their slaves free. As the president explained to Burton, all slaves over thirty-five years old would be freed at once; younger slaves would be freed in ten years. Congress would establish a fund of $900,000 that would be used to compensate slave masters, who would receive a generous payment of about $500 per slave. The cost for freeing the slaves of Delaware was less than the government spent on a single day of fighting the Confederacy. "This," Lincoln explained, "was the cheapest and most humane way of ending this war."[79]

As Fisher surely knew, the plan ignored the political realities in Delaware, whose residents had a deep-rooted aversion to outside meddling in state affairs. If the plan succeeded, the war could be ended, and Lincoln would emerge as a hero. If it failed, Fisher's political career in Delaware would be over.

President Lincoln as he appeared when he proposed his compensated emancipation plan. *Courtesy of the Delaware Public Archives.*

After Lincoln finished describing his proposal, Burton agreed to assist the president. As the largest slave owner in the state, Burton was convinced that the other slave owners of Delaware would recognize the favorable economics of the plan and react enthusiastically. When he returned home to Delaware and explained Lincoln's proposal of compensated emancipation to the coastal region's slave owners, however, Burton was stunned to learn that they did not share his enthusiasm for the proposal. Slave owners of southern Delaware considered the president's plan an unwarranted interference in their affairs, and they resented Lincoln's attempt to buy his way out of the Civil War. Despite the initial negative reaction to the plan encountered by Burton, Congressman Fisher persevered. He saw that a bill was introduced in the Delaware General Assembly that would put Lincoln's plan for compensated emancipation into motion. Although Fisher was able to convince some members of the General Assembly to support the proposal, the opposition was strong and vociferous. A resolution was introduced that maintained, "When the people of Delaware desire to abolish slavery within her borders, they will do so in their own way."[80] Opponents to ending slavery preyed on the fear that freeing the two thousand slaves in Delaware would add to the twenty thousand free African Americans and would constitute a dangerous threat to the white population. "In a short time, they might equal the white population and cause a massacre."[81] That concern was shared by some Republican abolitionists who were hostile to equal rights for African Americans. Delaware, they thought, was riding on the back of a tiger from which it dared not get off.[82]

When Fisher failed to garner support for the plan in the Delaware General Assembly, Lincoln's attempt to end the Civil War by compensated emancipation collapsed. For the president, the plan had been a bold attempt to end the bloodshed that was well worth the effort. For George Fisher, it was the end of his political career. In 1862, he was defeated for reelection. Although he would be appointed to a number of judicial positions, the courageous Fisher would not hold elected office again.[83]

Balloon over Sussex

All who submit peaceably to the authority of the Government are to be regarded as loyal.
—Major General John A. Dix

In Sussex County, Thomas B. Giles, Joseph Bacon, John S. Bacon and S.B. Frost were Southern sympathizers with military minds. In Europe, the use of balloons that were tethered to the earth by a strong rope had proven extremely valuable for military observations. Filled with hydrogen, observation balloons rose several hundred feet into the air and provided observers with a commanding view of enemy territory. The four men from Laurel knew that the Confederacy had no balloons or the means to produce them. For them, the course was clear: they would steal a balloon from the Union army.[84]

Before the men from southern Delaware were able to put their plan into action, the Union high command received a report of a plot to steal one of the Union's new observation balloons. Fearful that Delaware might join the rebelling states, Lincoln was reluctant to do anything that might drive the First State into the Confederacy. At the same time, the Federal leadership continued to receive reports of the activities of the Southern sympathizers of the Eastern Shore of Maryland and Virginia.

Several Union regiments, including the Second Delaware, which was composed of men who came from New Castle and Kent Counties, under Brigadier General Henry H. Lockwood were dispatched to communities in southern Delaware and on the Eastern Shore of Maryland and Virginia. Although Lockwood's primary mission was to secure the Eastern Shore of Virginia, he was also concerned with the Southern sympathizers in Maryland and Delaware. Because many residents in these areas were loyal to the Union, Lockwood was directed to act with some sensitivity and to disarm and disperse any militia groups that were dominated by Southern sympathizers. In addition, Lockwood was ordered to arrest anyone found to be in the service of the Confederacy. Although he was to be firm with those armed groups whose loyalty to the Union was doubtful, Lockwood would pursue a conciliatory course toward civilians. He was given specific authority to arrest any of his men who insulted civilians or damaged their property. The residents of Delaware, Maryland and Virginia were to be treated as citizens of the loyal Northern states: "All who submit peaceably to the authority of the Government are to be regarded as loyal." He was to use discretion and prudence so that "the people of these counties can be induced to declare their independence of the Confederates, the strongest assurance may be given to them of an efficient protection by the Government." Finally, Lockwood was to be on guard for surprise attacks: "It is understood that the intention is to carry on a guerrilla warfare against you, and that the character of the country favors it."[85]

Lockwood carried out the operation swiftly and efficiently. Some of the Southern sympathizers were roused out of bed at all hours of the night. Captain Moorehouse, with a detachment of the Second Delaware, arrived at the house of Benjamin Gunter of Accomack County, Virginia, at midnight. Awakened by the loud rapping at his door, Gunter recalled, "I arose from my bed went to my window and discovered that my house was surrounded with armed soldiers with guns at [the] ready."[86]

According to Gunter, he was immediately taken into custody. "[Moorehouse's] squad of men were then ordered to fall in and consisted as near as I could see of twenty-six privates two commissioned and one non-commissioned officer."[87] As the troops of the Second Delaware rode toward their camp with their prisoner, Gunter spoke to Moorehouse about the treatment of political prisoners and the conduct of the Union officers in making arrests. Moorehouse contended that the Union troops were being too benign in their treatment of Southern sympathizers, and he commented "that it was not in accordance with his opinions that they were treated too kindly, and denouncing them as traitors, rebels and using other hard epithets evidently intended to wound my feelings. I then a prisoner unarmed and in his hands and he surrounded by twenty-eight armed men."[88]

As the Union troops swept through Maryland and Virginia, Lockwood detached a company of the Second Delaware Regiment to Seaford, Laurel and Georgetown. Henry du Pont had written to Lockwood, "In regard to disarming certain other companies in this state, my view is that a citizen who is not loyal is not entitled to hold arms of the state." According to du Pont, a citizen's constitutional right to bear arms was based on the presupposition that he was loyal; if he became disloyal, he forfeited that as his right. Du Pont wrote to Lockwood, "I think that the disarming should be thorough making no exceptions."[89]

When Lockwood's force swept into Sussex County, they confiscated the weapons of southern Delaware militia companies that had demonstrated Confederate sympathies.

At Laurel, Lockwood's troops arrested Thomas B. Giles, Joseph Bacon, John S. Bacon and S.B. Frost, who had been implicated in the plot to steal a Union observation balloon. The four men from Laurel were hustled off to Northern prisons.[90] In addition, the incursion into southern Delaware deterred Southern sympathizers from using the coastal inlets as a conduit for war materiel.

Confederate Invasion

Sussex is sound to the core…We give secession and secessionists no quarter in this county.
—Caleb S. Layton

Sussex County was the most Southern in geography and spirit of Delaware's three counties. Nonetheless, in the center of Georgetown, the county seat, the Brick Hotel, across the green from the county courthouse, became a center for Union activity. In addition, Sussex County's two newspapers were both pro-Union. After Fort Sumter, the editor of the *Georgetown Messenger* advocated hanging secessionists. After a mob threatened to hang him, he moderated his stance somewhat.[91]

On the coast near Henlopen at the entrance to Delaware Bay, Lewes, nestled in the lee of Cape Henlopen, was a prime target for pirates, privateers and other sea-born marauders. Lewes had been established in the seventeenth century when most of inland Delaware was wilderness inhabited by Native Americans. The town near Cape Henlopen had a history of being attacked from the sea. During the colonial period, pirates ransacked Lewes, and throughout the American Revolution, the British Royal Navy harassed the inhabitants of the town. A generation later, during the War of 1812, a British flotilla anchored off Lewes and demanded supplies. When the plucky town refused, the British attacked Lewes with cannons and rockets. At the end of the twenty-four-hour bombardment, Lewes remained defiant. The British sailed away in disgust, prompting one budding poet to remark, "The commodore and all his men, shot a dog and killed a hen."[92]

Antique cannons reportedly used to defend Lewes during the War of 1812. *Courtesy of the Delaware Public Archives.*

In the opening weeks of the war, Henry F. Rodney, the president of the Lewes town commissioners, believed that there were few Southern sympathizers in the area. He wrote to Secretary of the Treasury Salmon P. Chase that the town was exposed to attack from the sea and asked for cannon to defend Lewes.[93] In the Lewes area, there were many people who had been quiet on the secession crisis who were now "ready, and willing to give their lives to the support of the right, and the perpetuity of our glorious institutions, and the putting down and forever quelling teas in high places and low."[94] Another prominent Republican, Caleb S. Layton, wrote, "Sussex is sound to the core…We give secession and secessionists no quarter in this county."[95] Union supporters in Sussex County met, and two militia companies were organized and seemed to be in firm control of the coastal region until July and the Battle of Bull Run.

The Confederate victory at Bull Run emboldened the secessionists in Delaware. A group of Southern sympathizers from Dover calling themselves the Peace Party boarded a steamer and headed for Lewes. After the steamer docked at Lewes, the secessionists spilled ashore and marched into town, where they cheered lustily for Jefferson Davis, the president of the Confederacy, and for General Beauregard, the victor of Bull Run. As the day wore on and some of the Southern sympathizers became intoxicated, the Confederate carousing grew more raucous. In addition to cheering for Davis and Beauregard, some of the Southerners declared that they were confirmed secessionists and they were determined to die for the Confederate cause.

The residents of Lewes, who generally opposed the Confederacy, were alarmed by the rowdy behavior of the Southern sympathizers. For most of the day, the people of Lewes were able to keep the boisterous secessionists somewhat in check, but after nightfall, additional Southern sympathizers arrived in town. Many of the reinforcements were armed, and after assembling on the banks of Lewes Creek, they began to march toward town.

In Lewes, an armed group of sailors assembled to meet the approaching mob of Southerners. Both groups appeared to be evenly matched, but the defenders of Lewes had an old six-pounder cannon that could inflict horrendous casualties on the Confederates with a single shot. When the two groups met, the Southerners continued to cheer for the Confederacy and hurl insults at the Lewes supporters of the Union. After the Southerners spotted the cannon, however, they recognized that any attack would be folly. The Confederates retreated to the dock, where they boarded a boat and sailed away.

Despite their boasts that they intended to return, Lewes was rid of the Southern sympathizers. The old cannon, however, remained in place, and it was fired to celebrate Northern victories. As the Civil War wore on, Southern sympathizers became tired of hearing the blasts of the old cannon, and they stole it and buried it on a farm on Pilottown Road.[96]

The Secret Mission of Lammot du Pont

You may stand for this but damned if I will.
—Lord Palmerston

"I was called to Washington," Henry du Pont wrote to his cousin, Captain Samuel Du Pont (Samuel spelled the family name with an uppercase D), "[and] had an interview with Secretary of State Seward and Secretary of War Simon Cameron." During the summer of 1861, the fighting had shown that the conflict would last longer, inflict more casualties and take more gunpowder than anticipated. Before Fort Sumter, Union stocks of powder were considered adequate to subdue the South, but now du Pont, Seward and Cameron were not so sure.[97]

Gunpowder in the nineteenth century was a mixture of 75 percent potassium nitrate (popularly known as saltpeter) and 25 percent a combination of sulphur and charcoal in approximately equal amounts. Charcoal and sulphur were readily available, but most of the world's saltpeter was supplied by India, which was under British control. Brokers in London or Liverpool, who purchased saltpeter from suppliers in Calcutta, ensured that the British dominated the saltpeter trade. If the Du Pont mills were to continue to produce gunpowder for the Union guns, a secure supply of saltpeter was needed.[98]

When Henry du Pont met with Secretaries Seward and Cameron, they decided to send an agent on a secret mission to Great Britain. The person selected for the mission had to be familiar with saltpeter, resourceful in international trade and sensitive to the diplomatic relationship between the United States and Great Britain, which the Confederates were also courting. Lammot du Pont was chosen for this important yet delicate mission, and on November 6, he set sail for Great Britain.

Lammot was born in 1831 and educated at the University of Pennsylvania, where he majored in chemistry. Entering the family business, he supervised the operations of the saltpeter refinery and laboratory work. He reportedly had run the allied blockade of Crimea with a boatload of powder for Russia during the Crimean War, and he spent three months in 1858 visiting powder mills and arsenals in Europe. A tall young fellow wearing spectacles, with a large mouth and a broad chin, Lammot walked clumsily but spoke well as befit a gentleman.[99]

Three days after Lammot left for Europe, a Union warship stopped a British steamer and arrested James Mason and John Slidell, two Confederate diplomats bound for Europe. The American public initially reacted with glee at this snub of Great Britain, and Lammot reached London before the news of the capture of Mason and Slidell arrived. Across the Atlantic, Henry du Pont wrote to Captain Samuel Du Pont that the saltpeter needed to be purchased and "shipped before any trouble may grow out of the seizure of Mason & Slidell."[100]

Authorized to buy a year's supply of saltpeter, du Pont immediately set to work buying the prime ingredient of gunpowder. He quickly bought up all that was available in England and contracted for more on board ships en route from India. Lammot charted four ships to carry the saltpeter to America, but these efforts came to an abrupt halt. When the news of the taking of Mason and Slidell reached England, the British press and public reacted angrily. Reacting to the impressment of the two Confederate diplomats from a British ship, Prime Minister Lord Palmerston declared to his cabinet, "You may stand for this but damned if I will."[101]

When the British government immediately placed an embargo on the shipment of saltpeter to America, Lammot tried to skirt the embargo by chartering ships to sail to France, where he planned to reship the saltpeter to America. Lammot was certain that England was preparing for war, and he left for America on December 7 and arrived home in Delaware on Christmas Day. He went to Washington the next day and reported to Secretary of State Seward. Determined to fight one war at a time, the Lincoln administration determined to release Mason and Slidell on the grounds that the captain who had detained them acted without orders. On January 1, 1862, the two Confederates were released and immediately booked passage on a ship for England. When Lammot learned that the diplomatic crisis had passed, he, too, headed for England, and as luck would have it, he sailed on the same ship as the Confederate diplomats. Unfortunately, no record of any of their conversations exists.

Du Pont arrived in London on January 13. Five days later, he received a note that stated, "The *prohibition* is removed—we are busy engaging freight."[102] Lammot began loading his stockpile of saltpeter for America, and two weeks later, he sailed for home, having shipped seven million pounds of saltpeter that could be used to manufacture nearly ninety-five thousand barrels of gunpowder, which was enough to carry on the war for another three years. When Lammot returned home in mid-February 1862, he resumed command of Company B of the local Brandywine Home Guard and returned to making gunpowder at the family firm.[103]

From the Front: Port Royal

I never hold councils of war.
—Rear Admiral Samuel F. Du Pont

While Lammot du Pont was setting out for Europe on his mission to buy saltpeter, Captain Samuel Francis Du Pont was leading a hastily assembled fleet southward along the Atlantic coast. A cousin of Henry du Pont, Samuel was born in 1803. He began a lifelong career in the United States Navy when he went to sea as a midshipman at the age of twelve. By the start of the Civil War, he had over four decades of experience in a variety of assignments on sea and land. In June 1861, Du Pont was a member of the Blockade Board that laid out the naval strategy for subduing the Confederacy, and as the first step in the strategy, Du Pont was appointed as flag officer of the South Atlantic Squadron, charged with blockading the Southern coast from Cape Henry to Key West.[104]

Admiral Samuel Francis Du Pont, the victor at Port Royal, South Carolina. *Courtesy of the Delaware Public Archives.*

On October 29, 1861, Flag Officer Du Pont left Hampton Roads with a fleet of fifty warships and army transport vessels.[105] His flagship was the steam frigate *Wabash*, built from the keel up as a naval warship, but many other vessels in the fleet were converted canalboats and steamships or hastily built "ninety-day gunboats." Du Pont commented that altering a steamer into a warship was like "altering a vest into a shirt." The new steam sloop-of war *Tuscarora* was built with such speed that Du Pont said, "Her keel was growing in Sussex County, Delaware, seventy days ago."[106] Despite the polyglot nature of his ships, Du Pont had assembled one of the most formidable fleets ever seen in American waters.

Successfully weathering a storm off Cape Hatteras, Du Pont's fleet sailed to Port Royal Sound, South Carolina, the target of his expedition. Port Royal Sound, off the northern edge of Hilton Head Island and southeast of Parris Island, was a fine natural anchorage, which the Lincoln administration envisioned as a base for the blockading squadron. The entrance to Port Royal was guarded by two earthen fortifications, Fort Beauregard on Bay Point on the north side of the channel and Fort Walker on Hilton Head to the south. In addition, a squadron of Confederate gunboats was stationed in the tributaries of Port Royal Sound.[107]

Du Pont arrived off the entrance to Port Royal on Monday, November 4. The next day, he "made a reconnaissance in force and drew the fire of the batteries on Hilton Head and Bay Point sufficiently to show that the fortifications were works of strength and scientifically constructed."[108] According to Du Pont, the forts "were armed with more than twenty guns each of the heaviest caliber and longest range, and were well constructed and well manned, but that the one on Hilton Head was the stronger."[109] He resolved to reduce Fort Walker on Hilton Head first and, when that was done, to take care of Fort Beauregard.

Traditionally, forts with several feet of earth to protect their cannon had an advantage over ships whose wooden sides were vulnerable to heavy shot and shell. Du Pont, however, devised a plan to take advantage of his ships' maneuverability. The distance of the channel between the two Confederate forts was over two nautical miles, and he ordered the line of attacking ships to steam down the middle of the channel, "receiving and returning the fire of both [forts]," as Du Pont put it. Once the Union warships were clear of the forts and driving the inconsequential Southern gunboats before them, the warships turned to the south and swung close past Fort Walker. When they were clear of the fort, the line of ships turned again and headed back into the entrance to Port Royal Sound. In effect, the maneuver formed a large oval that allowed the Union gunners to fire at the fixed Confederate positions. The Southern gunners, on the other hand, were faced with hitting a moving target.[110]

On the morning of November 7, Du Pont in the *Wabash* led the line of ships into the channel between the two forts, and at 9:26 a.m., the Confederates opened fire from Fort Walker. This was immediately followed by another shot from Fort Beauregard. The Southern shots were answered at once by the *Wabash*. A half hour later, the *Wabash* turned and slowly steamed past Fort Wagner at a range of about six hundred yards. As Du Pont completed one loop of his oval, the fire of the Northern warships had begun to rip Fort Walker apart. According to Du Pont, "It was evident that the enemy's fire was becoming much less frequent, and finally it was kept up at such long intervals and with so few guns as to be of little consequence."[111]

After Du Pont had taken possession of the Confederate batteries, he wrote to Gideon Welles, the secretary of the navy, "The defeat of the enemy terminated in utter rout and confusion…P.S.—The bearer of dispatches will also carry with him the first American ensign raised upon the soil of South Carolina since this rebellion broke out."[112]

Du Pont's victory at Port Royal earned him a promotion to rear admiral and the next task of attacking Charleston. It was not until April 1863 that the forces could be assembled to assault the cradle of the Confederacy. During that time, the epic encounter of the *Monitor* and the *Merrimack* had occurred, and there were those in the Navy Department who overestimated the capabilities of the new ironclads.[113] Although Du Pont had added eight ironclads to his fleet, the entrance to Charleston Harbor was heavily defended by batteries on the mainland and Fort Sumter, which sat in the center of the channel. Du Pont's initial attack on April 7, 1863, ended in failure. He reported, "I yesterday moved up with eight ironclads and this ship and attacked Fort Sumter…It was fierce and obstinate, and the gallantry of the officers and men of the vessels engaged was conspicuous."[114] Finding that the Union attack had not damaged the defenses of Charleston, Du Pont signaled the ships to withdraw, intending to renew the attack the next morning. When the commanders of the ironclad monitors came on board Du Pont's flagship, *New Ironsides*, they reported that five of the eight vessels had been seriously damaged.[115] Du Pont wrote to Secretary of the Navy Gideon Welles, "Without hesitation or consultation (for I never hold councils of war), I determined not to renew the attack, for, in my judgment, it would have converted a failure into a disaster."[116]

Almost immediately, stories critical of Du Pont's failure to take Charleston began to circulate in the newspapers, and the Lincoln administration was slow to defend the Delaware admiral. A colleague wrote, "Grieved by his unsuccessful effort to take that city, Admiral Du Pont was deeply pained by the attitude of the Navy Department toward him."[117] Du Pont was unceremoniously transferred to shore duty, and he played no other significant role in the war.

Chapter 3

Into the Fight

The Play's the Thing

The audience at the opening will be at once brilliant, engaging and no doubt attractive.
—New York Times

The hand-painted curtain rolled down to mark the end of the performance of *La Tour De Nesle*, and the four hundred people in Hopkinson Hall responded with loud applause. Behind the curtain, soldiers from the First Delaware Regiment shifted the scenery for the next presentation. As they did so, Sergeant Charles Schaffer and Sergeant Allen Tatem stepped in front of the curtain and sang:

Eighty years have rolled away since that bright heroic day.
When our fathers, in the fray, struck the conquering blow.

The song, dedicated to Millard Fillmore, was written in 1856, eighty years after the passage of the Declaration of Independence, featuring this rousing chorus:

Praise to them, the bold, who spoke.
Praise to them, the brave, who broke
Stem oppression's galling yoke,
Eighty years ago.[118]

HOPKINSON HALL

1st Regiment Delaware Volunteers

THE AMATEURS connected with this Regiment will give another one of their SELECT ENTERTAINMENTS, at the above Hall,

On Thursday and Friday Evenings, March 6th and 7th, 1862

On which occasion they will produce the Drama of

MICHAEL EARLE, OR THE MANIAC LOVER!

Together with the Laughable Farce of the

SPECTRE BRIDEGROOM:

OR, A GHOST IN SPITE OF HIMSELF.

MICHAEL EARLE!

CAST OF CHARACTERS:

Philip DeArville,	Lieut. J. P. Postles, Co. A
Stephen Girard,	Lieut. E. Alexander, Co. C
Miles Melville,	Adjt. W. P. Saville,
David,	Lieut. Jas. Rickards, Co. B
Andy Adze,	James McKee, Co. A
Michael, (the Maniac,)	Lieut. James A. Oates, Co. B
Mary Woodard,	N. P. Ecleston, Co. F
Julia Spring,	T. Maloney, Co. H
Dame Stapleton,	J. Pennington, Co. I

Villagers, by the Company.

BALLAD, BY - - SARG'T SHAFFER
DUETT, - - - - " A. & R. TATEM

SPECTRE BRIDEGROOM!

Nicodemus,	Lieut. Jas. A. Oates, Co B
Diggory,	" Jas. Rickards, Co B
Squire Alwinkle,	A. Lockwood, Co A
Capt. Vauntington,	Adjt. W. P. Saville,
Paul,	James McKee, Co A
Thomas,	A. Vasey, Co F
Lavinia,	N. P. Ecleston, Co F
Georgiana,	G. Maloney, Co H

DOORS OPEN AT 6½ O'CLOCK. CURTAIN RISES AT 7.

The First Delaware printed impressive handbills for its theatrical productions. *Courtesy of the Delaware Public Archives.*

With lines like "There shall valor's work be done: like the sire shall be the son, Where the fight was waged and won" and "Hearts and hands shall guard those rights, bought on Freedom's battle heights" that were sure to stir any Union soldier's heart, "Eighty Years Ago" was a surefire crowd pleaser. After their duet was completed, the curtain rose on the evening's second presentation, a farce entitled *B.B., or the Benecia Boy in England.*[119]

Many Delaware colonists, especially the Quakers, had a strong aversion to the theater, which they considered to be an evil intrusion on the good work of daily life. In the early nineteenth century, Wilmington lacked a resident theater. Traveling theatrical companies, often based in Philadelphia, performed in the Wilmington area, but to avoid arousing Wilmington's anti-theatrical residents, these performances routinely were presented at the edge of town. Vandever's Tavern, at the borough line and Kennett Turnpike, hosted several performances in 1827. These traveling companies often staged Shakespeare, circuses and other forms of entertainment. Wilmington's leaders responded with an ordinance that levied a fifty-dollar fine for any circus performance, trick riding, exhibition, tumblers or puppet shows. Eventually, the religious and legal opposition was overcome, and in 1834, a theater opened at Front and Orange Streets. By the time the war had begun, most Delaware residents had accepted theatrical presentations as legitimate entertainment.[120]

In February 1862, when the First Delaware Regiment was stationed at Camp Hamilton near Fort Monroe, Virginia, Lieutenants James Oates and James Rickards of Company B came to the conclusion that the tedium of drill and guard duty had taken its toll. They believed a theater would help revive the morale of the Delaware troops and other members of the Northern forces.[121]

The troops from the First Delaware Regiment spent several weeks constructing an elaborate theater with seats for four hundred people, which included forty seats that were set aside for enlisted men. Each company commander was given ten tickets to distribute to enlisted men who were outstanding in the performance of their duties. The auditorium contained a large stage that was lit by footlights that were capable of providing different shades of light, an enclosure for an orchestra, chandeliers with tin sconces to hold the candles to light the auditorium and a tastefully furnished green room behind the stage. The First Delaware secured costumes from Baltimore, and to give the performances a professional setting, the Boothenian Dramatic Association of Wilmington sent some of the backgrounds down the Delmarva Peninsula. Although several ladies had volunteered to be actresses, all the roles would be played by males. The *New York Times*, in a review of the theater, reported that "it was determined that the former [ladies] would better grace the audience than the stage; and as there are some fifty ladies at Camp Hamilton, and all have promised to be present, the audience at the opening will be at once brilliant, engaging and no doubt attractive."[122]

The Delaware troops named their theater Hopkinson Hall in honor of popular Lieutenant Colonel Oliver P. Hopkinson. The first event in the new theater was a ball hosted by the regiment's officers. Invitations were sent to the officers in the Union army and to the officers of a French war vessel that was anchored near Fort Monroe. In addition, some of the mischievous Delaware troops decided to extend an invitation to Confederate general John Magruder, an aficionado of the theater known as "Prince John" before the war.[123] According to William Seville, the Delaware regiment's historian, "Some of the wags amused themselves by nailing to a tree outside the picket-line a paper containing an invitation to General Magruder and staff to attend this ball, which, they said, as a polite recognition of General Magruder's attentions to us, by sending a flag of truce regularly once a week summing us to surrender Fort Monroe forthwith or remain in it at our peril."[124]

On February 17, 1862, the Delaware troops presented their first entertainment:

> *The audience which assembled to honor this first representation was, to use the well-worn phraseology of the newspapers, a large, fashionable, and intelligent one, embracing as it did all the officers of the fort and camp not on duty, with many ladies; and loud and earnest were the plaudits bestowed on the enterprising members of the Delaware Regiment for such a valuable contribution to the amusements of camp-life.*[125]

A few weeks after opening night for Hopkinson Hall, on Thursday and Friday, March 6 and 7, the First Delaware actors presented *Michael Earle, or the Maniac Lover!* together with the laughable farce of the *Spectre Bridegroom: Or, a Ghost in Spite of Himself. Michael Earle* had been produced in Chicago and was produced periodically from time to time, with one production starring the renowned Jenny Lin.[126] In the First Delaware's production, Lieutenant Postles played Philip DeAvrville, Lieutenant Rickards played Miles Melville and Lieutenant Oates played the title role, Michael (the Maniac), while enlisted men were cast in the female or villager roles. In the *Spectre Bridegroom*, Oates, Rickards and Seville played prominent roles. Sergeants Shaffer and Tatem reprised their duet:

> *Pour the wine of sacrifice*
> *Let the grateful anthem rise*
> *Shall we e'er resign the prize?*
> *Never—never—no!*
> *Hearts and hands shall guard these rights,*
> *Bought on Freedom's battle heights,*
> *Where he fixed his signal lights,*
> *Eighty years ago!*[127]

From the Front: The *Monitor* and the *Merrimack*

The men laughed and shouted to see the little thing fight.
—Chaplin Thomas G. Murphey

While the presentations in Hopkinson Hall were lifting the spirits of the troops, another drama was playing out in the waters off Delaware. The wind was moderate off the Delaware coast, but it freshened to a strong breeze from the northwest and caused a rough sea, which the newly constructed *Monitor* encountered while it was being towed from New York to Hampton Roads, Virginia. The waves broke over the vessel's low deck, forcing water through the hawse pipes and under the turret. During the afternoon, the waves increased and broke over the smoke pipe and blower pipe, threatening to end its rendezvous with the CSS *Virginia.*

Aboard the storm-stricken *Monitor*, broken blower bands stopped the draft in the furnace, and the engine room and fire room filled with dangerous gases. Several of the crewmen collapsed, fortunately being saved by other quick-thinking crewmen who dragged them out of the engine room to fresh air.

By this time, all power had been lost, and the *Monitor*'s engines were now useless. The crew manned the hand pump and set up a bucket brigade to fight the tide of rising water on the iron ship. The vessel's radically low freeboard prevented the sailors from making much headway. After battling the heavy waves for five hours, the storm subsided, and the smoother water enabled the engine room to be cleared of gas. The blower bands were repaired, and the engine again became operational.

After midnight, the Monitor was hit with another storm. The sea broke again over the deck, and the water again entered the blower pipes. In addition to taking on more water, the steering mechanism became jammed. The vessel was now unmanageable, beginning to dip and rise wildly in the waves straining the towropes that tethered the *Monitor* to its tug. The lines held, and after five critical hours, daylight broke. By eight o'clock, the danger was over. At four o'clock in the afternoon on March 8, the *Monitor* passed Cape Henry, where the hawsers parted, but the vessel was now in smooth water and out of danger.[128]

Having survived the storm off the Delaware coast, the *Monitor* steamed under its own power into Hampton Roads, where the crew on the ironclad was greeted by a scene of sunken and burning ships. Fresh from their theatrical performance, the troops crowded onto rooftops and watched as the *Virginia* steamed into Hampton Roads. The *Virginia* had begun life as the steam frigate *Merrimack*, scuttled by the Union forces when they abandoned Norfolk early in the war. The resourceful Confederates had salvaged the hull, patched up the engines and built a barn-like structure of iron on the rejuvenated frigate, which they christened *Virginia*. Despite the name change, many in the North continued to refer to the Southern ironclad as the *Merrimack*.

On March 8, the *Virginia* entered Hampton Roads to engage the entire Union fleet and lift the Union stranglehold on the Chesapeake Bay. The Union troops, including the soldiers from Delaware, had heard rumors that something was afoot, and they crowded onto trees, rooftops and other lofty perches to get a good view of the action. Around noon, a mysterious-looking craft that resembled a huge roof came from the direction of Norfolk and proceeded toward two of the Union wooden warships, the *Cumberland* and *Congress*, anchored together off Newport News. Word quickly spread through the gawking Union troops that the odd-shaped vessel was the ironclad *Virginia*. Rumor had it that the Confederate ironclad would "crush our men-of-war like egg-shells and capture all our seaports, finishing with the Federal capital."[129]

Captain Seville of the First Delaware recalled, "We witnessed this maritime monster ram to destruction those two noble vessels, the *Cumberland* and the *Congress* treating with utter contempt the shower of heavy shot that was poured against her iron ribs." After disposing of these two warships, the *Virginia* headed for the *Minnesota*, which had grounded in water too shallow to permit the Confederate ironclad to approach the Union vessel. Having proven that it was superior to any wooden warship afloat, the *Virginia* steamed triumphantly back to Norfolk "as the shadow of evening were falling on the burning wreck of the *Congress* and the shattered spars of the *Cumberland* projecting but a few feet above the surface of the water, with the stars and stripes still floating from the mast."[130]

News of the Confederate ironclad's victory was telegraphed to Washington, where Lincoln's cabinet was driven into a frenzy. Secretary of War Edwin Stanton was worried that "the *Merrimack*...would destroy every vessel in the service, could lay every city on the coast under contribution, could take Fortress Monroe; McClellan's mistaken purpose to advance by the Peninsula must be abandoned." Lincoln and his advisors were afraid that the Confederate warship would sail up the Potomac, disperse Congress, destroy the capital and continue up the coast to destroy the other Northern cities.[131]

The next morning, the Delaware troops climbed again into their vantage points amid rumors that an ironclad called the *Monitor* had arrived to do battle with the *Virginia*. At the first streak of dawn, thousands of anxious eyes swept the broad expanse of water in search of the promised savior, but the troops could find nothing that bore the slightest resemblance to an ironclad capable of doing battle with the *Virginia*, which was steaming into Hampton Roads.[132]

As the Rebel ironclad steamed toward the grounded *Minnesota* to administer the coup de grâce, the Delaware troops heard a muffled report from a cannon and observed a puff of white smoke far off in the direction of Pig Point, "surmounted by what seemed to be a black bandbox."[133] As the "black bandbox" drew closer, the Delaware troops saw a vessel "of more novel appearance and singular construction…slipping down quietly from the direction of Newport News, and boldly approaching the great giant. It was the *Monitor*!"[134] Chaplin Thomas G. Murphey of the First Delaware saw the encounter between the two warships in biblical terms: "Then she announced herself as a champion of the stars and stripes, and accepted the challenge of the Confederate Goliath, as David, the shepherd boy of Israel, accepted that of the proud Philistine."[135]

A thrill of joy ran through the ranks of the First Delaware. Moving backward and forward with equal ease, the *Monitor* dodged the shells from the *Virginia*, and at the same time, the Union ironclad's revolving turret enabled it to always be in position for delivering a shot. The Delaware troops "laughed and shouted to see the little thing fight. We felt that our cause was safe."[136]

Neither ironclad was able to do material damage to the other, but the balance of power had shifted back to the North. The threat of the *Virginia* terrorizing Washington, D.C., and other Northern cities was over. The *Monitor* had successfully survived a winter storm along the Delaware coast to rendezvous with the *Virginia* in time.

Chaplain Thomas G. Murphey viewed the battle of the *Monitor* and the *Virginia* as a contest between David and Goliath. *Courtesy of the Delaware Public Archives.*

Underground Railroad Runs in Reverse

These soldiers were stationed at the depot to intercept suspicious characters.
—*Henry Hollyday*

"In the summer of 1862...citizens...of the United States...were exercised over a draft," as Henry Hollyday, a Southern sympathizer from the Eastern Shore of Maryland, explained years later, "which had been called by President Lincoln, to fill up the decimated ranks of the 'Union' or 'Northern Army.'"[137] Hundreds of Maryland and Delaware Southerners were appalled that they would be forced to fight for the Union. They left their homes to make their way south to enlist in the Confederate army.[138]

In order to reach Confederate-held territory, Hollyday left Maryland and crossed into Delaware north of Dover. From the Delaware state capital, he followed, in reverse, the route that Harriet Tubman and other fugitive slaves had taken to reach freedom. In September 1862, he met with relatives and friends at his old family mansion on the Chester River, where a companion agreed to accompany him on his flight south. As the two Southern sympathizers prepared for their journey to join the Confederate forces, they had to be careful not arouse suspicion, Hollyday thought, because some of the house servants were "supporters of the Northern cause, who were ever seeking an opportunity to entrap Southern Sympathizers."[139]

After "an ample supply of gold and a limited supply of clothing" had been packed, the two men set out. Unlike the fugitive slaves who traveled in the dark of night, Hollyday hired a trusted hand to drive him and his compatriot to Smyrna, Delaware, "where a staunch Southern Sympathizer would entertain them."[140] Following the course of the Chester River eastward, the two men reached Smyrna about sundown and stayed with the "staunch Southern Sympathizer," who was a volunteer agent of the reverse (as Hollyday styled it) "underground route."[141]

The agent advised Hollyday and his friend on the safest route to Dover, which they reached around noon that day. Fortunately, a political convention was being held in the state capital, and strangers from all parts of Delaware were in attendance. The two Confederate sympathizers had no trouble blending in with the throng of political visitors. The train for Seaford did not leave until 3:00 p.m., and the pair spent their time at the convention, visiting the state buildings and dining at a hotel.

As the time approached to catch the train for Seaford, Hollyday and his friend walked over to the depot, where they spotted a number of soldiers of

The public square at Dover was the center of political affairs. *Courtesy of the Delaware Public Archives.*

PENINSULAR

RAIL ROAD LINE.

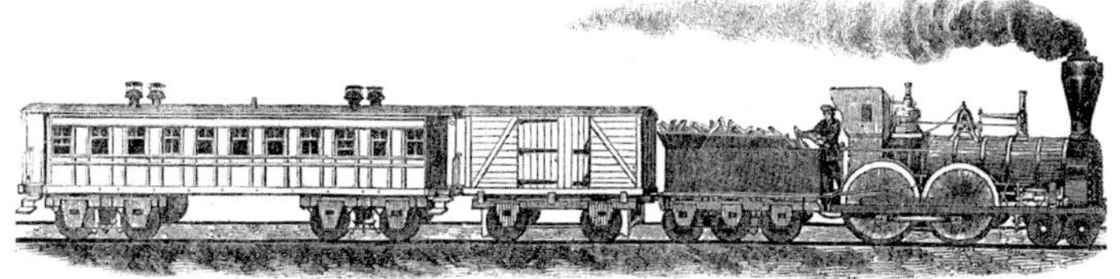

CHANGE OF HOURS.

On and after Monday, January 5th, 1863,

Henry Hollyday rode in style aboard the train in the reverse underground railroad. *Courtesy of the Delaware Public Archives.*

the provost guards who were watching to intercept any suspicious characters. Acting as naturally as they could, the two men passed the guards and boarded the train. As Hollyday recalled, the provost guards did not "realize, that the train as it started off southward, contained two Rebels aboard. Great was the relief of our travelers when they found the train rapidly carrying them away from immediate danger."[142]

At sundown, the train chugged into Seaford, and as the two Southern sympathizers disembarked, they deemed it prudent to ascertain how the local inhabitants felt about "this great contest, for there was scarcely one man, woman, or child throughout the entire land, who had not become identified in some way with one or other of the contending forces."[143] Fortunately, Hollyday met an elderly gentleman who was in sympathy with the South, and the man directed Hollyday to a friendly house where the two men enjoyed "a first rate supper."[144]

From Seaford, the two men headed southwest roughly following the course of the Nanticoke River. After passing Johnson's Crossroads, where, a generation earlier, the notorious Patty Cannon had kidnapped an untold number of African Americans and sold them into slavery, Hollyday was able to make his way down the Nanticoke River and across the Chesapeake Bay to Virginia, where he enlisted in the Confederate army.[145] Although he had followed much the same path taken by the fugitive slaves in the years before the Civil War, Henry Hollyday had traveled in the daytime, rode openly on the train and dined in a hotel on the "reverse underground railroad."

From the Front: Antietam

Do it and I will get there!
—Lieutenant Charles Tanner

At the end of the summer of 1862, the war was a year old, and the Delaware troops had not yet fought in battle. During their first year of service, the First Delaware Regiment was confined to guarding railroad bridges, putting on theatrical performances and watching the epic battle between the *Monitor* and the *Merrimack*. After a year of service, the First Delaware had not fired a shot in anger, and several of the unit's officers petitioned the Union high command for the regiment to be assigned to front-line duty. On September 5, 1862, General Joseph Mansfield summed up the First Delaware's service to that point: "Well drilled, and been in service for about fourteen months and have never fired a gun at the enemy."[146]

For the men of the First Delaware, the war had become a series of spectacles and grand parades. According to one of the regiment's officers, "Our dress-parades had become a fine military pageant to the other regiments of the brigade, some of which changed the time for their own evening parade to a later hour that they might have the opportunity to witness ours."[147]

When President Lincoln arrived to inspect the Union forces in the Tidewater area of Virginia, he reviewed the troops, and the Delaware soldiers were determined to "make as imposing a martial appearance as possible." Drum Major Patrick Dooley, who wore "the tallest and most gorgeous of shakoes,"[148] led the regimental band across the front of the regiment. President Lincoln quietly inspected the Delaware troops as he rode behind the band. When the first members of the band reached the end of the regiment, the musicians turned about smartly. Drum Major Dooley, strutting with his shoulders back, marched smartly through the musicians to take his place at the head of the line, when he suddenly came face to face with the president in front of a cadre of horsemen. Both men came to a dead halt. There sat the embarrassed president, motionless on his horse, and there stood Dooley with his glittering staff held at a forty-five-degree angle across his chest and standing firm as the rock of Gibraltar. Behind Dooley, the band did not miss a beat and blared away while marking time. "After a few moments of hesitation, which provoked a hearty peal of laughter from all, the President…opened the road for Dooley and the band out of their dilemma."[149]

The Union high command may not have trusted the loyalty of troops from a slave state, but on September 8, 1862, the troops of the First Delaware were ordered onto steamers for a quick trip to Washington, D.C. When Major General John Dix detached the First Delaware and two other regiments from his command, he wrote to his superior in Washington, "You are perhaps not aware that these regiments are the flower of [my] command."[150]

From the nation's capital, the First Delaware marched westward as part of Major General George McClellan's Army of the Potomac that was preparing to meet General Robert E. Lee's Army of Northern Virginia, which had crossed the Potomac River into Maryland. In addition to the First Delaware, there were two other First State regiments in McClellan's Army. The Second Delaware, recruited during the summer of 1861, had already seen service as part of Brigadier General Lockwood's force that swept into the Delmarva Peninsula to suppress Southern sympathizers; and the Third Delaware, which contained men from Kent and Sussex Counties, was formed in the spring of 1862.[151]

Officers of the Third Delaware Infantry. *Courtesy of the Delaware Public Archives.*

As McClellan's army moved toward western Maryland to do battle with Lee, Wilmington was in an uproar. On September 12, 1862, the *Delaware State Journal and Statesman* announced, "TO ARMS! TO ARMS! Great War Meeting."[152]

On the same day that the First Delaware Regiment boarded the transports for the quick trip to Washington, D.C., residents of Wilmington gathered at city hall in response to a proclamation by Mayor Henry B. Judd. News of Lee's advance into Maryland had rippled eastward, and there were few troops to defend Wilmington. An immense crowd assembled at city hall to hear speeches by some of Delaware's fervent Union men calling for the organization of militia companies to defend the city and state from Rebel invasion. According to the *Delaware State Journal and Statesman*, the people of Wilmington's "hearts were in the cause; and that come weal or woe, they are now determined to fight to the 'bitter end' the enemies of popular government and human liberty."[153]

At city hall, a resolution was adopted to "put down the most gigantic, wicked, and heartless rebellion that ever disgraced humanity, and now seeks to destroy the best government on the face of the earth." In addition, the meeting called for the formation of the National Guard of Delaware to defend the state against the Rebels.[154]

A week after the Wilmington meeting, the three Delaware regiments were part of the Union army outside the town of Sharpsburg, Maryland, near Antietam Creek. Around daybreak on September 17, the right flank of the Union forces attacked Lee's army. In the confused fighting that was characteristic of the Battle of Antietam, the lines of evenly organized troops threatened to break down and turn the Union army into a milling mob of ineffective soldiers. The danger was avoided when "the old regiments, however, deployed promptly, and the new regiments (both officers and men of which behaved with marked coolness) soon got into line of battle, with more promptitude than could have been expected."[155] The Third Delaware fought hard and sustained a number of casualties until the action shifted eastward, where the First and Second Delaware Regiments were stationed a short distance from each other.

The First Delaware was advancing through a cornfield when it was attacked by a brisk fire from artillery and small arms. When the men reached the edge of the field, the path of the Delaware troops was barred by a post and rail fence. Although they were under a galling fire, the men scaled the fence, re-formed their line and moved rapidly forward.[156] As the Delaware troops continued to move ahead, they were confronted by the Confederates in two lines of battle, posted in a road or ravine four feet below the surface

A modern view of the Antietam battlefield where the Delaware troops saw their first major action. *Photo by Michael Morgan.*

of the adjoining field, with a third line in a field in the rear. The height of ground enabled the third line to fire over the heads of those in the ravine.[157]

According to one of the officers, "The fire the enemy was thus able to bring to bear on our single line was so destructive that even veteran troops would have been repulsed." The line of Delaware troops was staggered and recoiled, and the right of the regiment was forced back to the edge of the cornfield.[158] By this time, the regiment had lost a third of its men, and eight company commanders were either killed or wounded.[159]

Despite having taken these casualties, the regiment rallied and returned the enemy's fire with telling effect. In the no-man's land between the armies lay many of the killed and wounded of the First Delaware. In addition, two regimental colors, the symbol of pride and the unit's identity, lay on the ground between the lines of firing soldiers. The First Staters were mortified to discover the sight of two of the flags on the ground in front of the sunken road. Men began to creep forward to retrieve the flags, but most were driven back by the relentless fire of the Confederates. Finally, Sergeant Tatem, who had sung "Eighty Years Ago" in the spring, was able to retrieve one of the flags. Major Thomas A. Smyth began organizing a squad of sharpshooters to provide covering fire for another attempt to recover the second banner. Looking for a volunteer, the major asked Lieutenant Charles Tanner of Company H if he would rescue the flag when Smyth's squad was assembled. Tanner replied, "Do it and I will get there!"

Tanner crept forward through enemy fire. As he reached the fallen banner, a Confederate bullet struck him in the right arm. Without hesitating, Tanner snatched the colors from the ground and began a long dash toward Union lines. During his sprint with the flag, he was hit twice more but returned to the regiment with the colors in hand. For this exploit, Tanner was awarded the Medal of Honor.[160]

While the colors were being saved, a wounded Confederate began to hobble across the field. The man was spotted by Sergeant John Dunn. A native of Dublin, Ireland, Dunn had been an apprentice carriage trimmer in Wilmington before the war. As the Rebel made his way across the field, Dunn lifted his musket and exclaimed, "I'll drop that fellow."

Captain James Rickards was next to Dunn, and he pushed the sergeant's weapon down. Rickards said, "You wouldn't shoot a wounded man!" As soon as the officer had uttered the words, the Confederate quickly brought up his weapon and shot Rickards, who died almost instantly. The other Delaware troops who were watching the exchange responded with an immediate volley that killed the ungrateful Confederate.[161]

While they continued to fight, the men of the First Delaware hugged the ground to avoid the murderous fire of the Confederates. Eventually, reinforcements arrived and drove off the Southerners. A little to the east, the Second Delaware's experience was similar to the First Delaware's. The First Staters attacked and the Confederates counterattacked, but the Delaware men held their ground despite taking heavy casualties.[162]

When Antietam's bloody day had concluded, Anna Ferris summed up the feelings of many in the First State: "The horrors of the war oppress every one, [who]…wait with fear & dread for the tidings of our losses & grow sick at the sight of the long lists of the dead & wounded."[163] The list of the dead and wounded from Antietam was indeed long and numbered over three hundred Delaware men killed and wounded. The people of Wilmington were particularly saddened by the deaths of Captain Rickards and Captain Evan S. Watson, who had been in Wilmington when Lee invaded Maryland. Watson hurried to western Maryland and joined the Delaware troops in time for the battle. As he led his company into action, "he fell while gallantly encouraging his men in the advance."[164]

The bodies of Rickards and Watson reached Wilmington just before noon on Saturday, September 27, and the caskets were escorted from the railroad station to city hall by a detachment of the Fourth Delaware Regiment. The bodies lay in state at city hall until Monday shortly after three o'clock, when the coffins were placed in hearses and "the cortege began to move to the solemn music of the dead march." At city hall, the hearses were escorted by Delaware soldiers who silently wheeled into platoons as the procession began. An immense crowd, rivaling the one that had sent the First Delaware off to war over a year earlier, had gathered to witness the funeral procession as it made its way to Wilmington and Brandywine Cemetery. Many stores and businesses were closed during the afternoon, when "the bells tolled out their doleful music, [and] solemnity pervaded the streets."[165]

First Arrivals at Fort Delaware

I understand that Fort Delaware could very promptly and economically be fitted up for 200 prisoners by simply flooring the casemates.
—Major General John A. Dix

The smiling passengers toting baskets packed with picnic lunches marched down the gangplank from the steamboat and stepped ashore on Pea Patch

Island. After the development of steamboats, excursion boats flourished on the Delaware River. In 1824, steamboat service was opened to Cape May, a budding ocean resort, and by the 1850s, many people of Wilmington and Philadelphia looking to take excursions did not need to go to the mouth of the Delaware Bay. A dozen miles below Wilmington, Pea Patch Island had more than enough sights to satisfy nineteenth-century tourists.[166]

When William Penn acquired Delaware, he had an eye toward protecting his Pennsylvania colony and its principal city, Philadelphia. During the American Revolution and the War of 1812, the British Royal Navy had free reign of the Delaware River and menaced towns from Philadelphia to Lewes. Little thought was given to protecting Delaware towns. Lewes was too small and too exposed to consider, Dover was set back from the river and New Castle and Wilmington fell under the umbrella of Philadelphia. The natural location for a fortification was Pea Patch Island, which sat in the middle of the river near the eastern terminus of the Chesapeake and Delaware Canal at Delaware City.

Legend has it that Pea Patch Island began to form before the American Revolution when a boat with a cargo of peas wrecked on a shoal near a bend in the Delaware River. The hull of the ship was left to rot on the shoal, and the ship's cargo of peas took root, collected sediment and began to grow. Although in the 1770s it was said to be no larger than a hat, two decades later, in 1794, Pea Patch had grown to sufficient size that Major Pierre L'Enfant, who had laid out the streets of Washington, D.C., recommended building a fort on the muddy island.[167]

Nothing was done until after the War of 1812, when the first fortification was built. A disastrous fire and problems with the early fortification's foundation led to that fort being scrapped, and a new one was proposed to take its place. Then things got ugly. When the border between Delaware and New Jersey was laid out in the seventeenth century, Pea Patch Island did not exist. Although it was recognized that the border of Delaware extended in a twelve-mile radius from the New Castle Courthouse, it was not agreed that the circle extended over the Delaware River. The question had not raised any serious controversy until Pea Patch Island grew to a significant size. The ownership case dragged on through the courts, which confirmed Delaware's belief in the Union that protected it from a land grab by New Jersey. In 1843, Senator James Buchanan argued that the Federal government had selected Pea Patch Island for the site of a major fortification because it was a suitable place for the defense of the Delaware River. Buchanan contended that this Pea Patch Island was "a place material to the whole Union" and "the

Government was not to let a great commercial city be without its necessary defense, pending any controversy about State jurisdiction or individual right of title."[168]

Eventually, the case was settled enough to allow construction to begin. On a map, Pea Patch Island looked like the ideal spot to build a fort, but the grassy sandbar extended only a few feet above the water. In extremely high tides, the island was overrun with water. Bulkheading built by the army helped some, but the problem would be persistent. The plans called for a massive fort that would eventually mount 150 guns and have a garrison of 800, and it would be the largest constructed by the United States Army.[169] To support a masonry fort built on sand, using four steam-driven pile drivers, more than six thousand piles, forty-five feet long, were driven into the island.[170] Next, a grillage—a framework to spread the weight of the fort—had to be assembled. This preliminary work took until 1852 to complete, and the following spring, the first blocks of stone began to arrive. By then, Pea Patch had developed into a town with more than two hundred workers and their families living on the island.[171]

The piles of stones and the temporary houses of the workers looked like something from the Middle Ages. Although steam power was employed to do some of the heavy lifting, much of the stonework was done by hand hammers, chisels, levels, squares and other tools that were employed five hundred years ago. In addition, the archaic terminology of castles was employed—counterscarp, parapet, terreplein, embrasures, casemates—and as the fort began to rise, people of Wilmington and Philadelphia boarded excursion boats to see for themselves the wonder of army construction. The crowds gawked at the sheer size of the fort and marveled at the intricate system to catch rainwater and provide indoor plumbing for the garrison. In the unlikely event that Fort Delaware was put under a medieval siege, it could survive for up to four months.[172] Throughout the late 1850s, as the two levels of casemates rose over the Delaware River, the sightseeing business thrived. Wilmington and Philadelphia residents packed picnic lunches and boarded steamers for Pea Patch Island.[173]

At the start of 1861, when Delaware was considering the Southern overtures to join the Confederacy, the fort on Pea Patch Island was ready for the installation of its guns that would transform Fort Delaware into a modern installation.[174] In February of that year, Captain Augustus A. Gibson, a West Point veteran, class of 1839, took command of the meager garrison of twenty men at Fort Delaware. With just a fraction of the projected garrison, Gibson set about the task of mounting the guns and putting the fort on a war footing.

In this postwar photograph, steamboats line the Christina River in Wilmington. *Courtesy of the Delaware Public Archives.*

On April 24, 1861, after the firing on Fort Sumter, Major General Robert Patterson reported to the War Department, "Captain Gibson reported last week that he was able to hold Fort Delaware, but requested that the remainder of his company be directed to join him. I have detailed one hundred men (raw volunteers) to be placed under his command."[175] The sightseers continued to stop at Pea Patch Island. For a time, the garrison consisted of a regiment of Zuoaves, and the troops in their colorful uniforms added to the spectacle of a visit to the fort. In July 1861, sightseers were given an added reason to visit Fort Delaware when the first captured Confederate soldiers arrived.[176]

With the growing number of prisoners of war and the arrest of Southern sympathizers, the Union high command cast about for places to confine prisoners. Forts—such as Fort McHenry in Baltimore and Fort Warren in Boston Harbor—seemed like natural choices, but Fort McHenry, located in a city brimming with Southern sympathizers, was filling up with political prisoners, and General Dix was looking for another place to house them. On September 8, 1861, Dix wrote to the War Department, "I understand that Fort Delaware could very promptly and economically be fitted up for 200 prisoners by simply flooring the casemates."[177]

A modern photograph of Fort Delaware casemates that were converted to house prisoners. *Photo by Michael Morgan.*

In the ensuing weeks, captured Confederates and political prisoners began to arrive at Fort Delaware, but the tourists who continued to visit Pea Patch Island sometimes outnumbered the prisoners. When someone spiked a gun and helped a prisoner escape, Dix curtly wrote to the commander of the fort, Captain A.A. Gibson, "Put a stop at once to the visits of pleasure parties to the fort…We have lost one of our most important ones [prisoners] within a few days and have no doubt his escape was facilitated by communications between him and his friends."[178] The tourists were expelled from the island, the fort took on a more military look and the prisoners continued to arrive.

Election of 1862

There can be no doubt, I think, about that being the object.
—Shepherd P. Houston

Representative George Fisher was worried. In 1862, he was up for reelection, but the numbers did not add up. Fisher, who had played a pivotal role in Lincoln's ill-fated plan for compensated emancipation, wrote to the president, "I deem it my duty to say that we have but 16,000 voters in the state all told; and of them we have sent already 2,000 men into the field. The present arrangement will diminish our strength from 500 to 1000 votes. Two years ago I had only a plurality of 247 votes. You may very readily see how slim will be our chances to carry the election."[179]

In Delaware's first statewide election to be held after the war had begun, Fisher's Republican Party styled itself the Union Party in the hope that it could attract Democrats who had voted for Stephen Douglas in 1860. In addition to nominating Fisher for Delaware's lone congressional seat, the Republicans selected William Cannon, a farmer, banker, merchant and political veteran, as the party's nominee for governor. Cannon was reputed to be the richest man in Sussex County, and on three previous occasions, he had tried to secure the Democratic nomination for governor and failed. Devoted to the Union, he took up the Republican mantle in 1862 with vigor. But Lincoln's issuance of the preliminary Emancipation Proclamation stirred the fires of racial politics.[180]

William Cannon was elected governor of Delaware in 1862. *Courtesy of the Delaware Public Archives.*

When Governor Burton did not seek reelection, the Democrats selected as their gubernatorial candidate Samuel Jefferson, a prominent New Castle County Democrat. To oppose Fisher in the race for Delaware's seat in the House of Representatives, the Democrats nominated William Temple, who, at age thirty-one, had become the youngest governor in Delaware history after Governor Joseph Muall died in 1846. Temple had been president of the Delware Senate, and after completing Muall's term, he returned to the Senate, only to emerge as a leader of the Constitutional Union Party in 1860.[181]

The Democratic platform declared that the people of Delaware alone should decide the issue of slavery, and the Democrats styled their opponents as the "Black-Republican-Abolition-Disunion Party," whose aim was "to place the negro on a footing of equality with the white man…and that they are prepared to degrade the white race to a level with the negroes at the bidding of false philanthropy and fanatical madness."[182]

Like Fisher, the Democrats had arithmetic on their minds when Samuel Townsend, who had engaged in fisticuffs at the Democratic convention in 1860, claimed that freeing the nearly two thousand slaves in Delaware would lead to a surge in the African American population that would result in a massacre of the state's white residents. Townsend pleaded with the former Douglas supporters to reject the Union (Republican) Party: "For God's sake unite with any party that will ward off this abolition blow."[183]

Republicans were equally vitriolic, claiming that the opposition were, in effect, traitors: "This the mis-called Democratic Party of this state is in earnest sympathy with this rebellion; that it has abandoned all principles of true Democracy; that it seeks, under the specious cry of peace, to recognize the so-called Southern Confederacy."[184]

As election day neared, Cannon and Fisher reported to Secretary of War Edwin Stanton and President Lincoln that Southern sympathizers were threatening to use violence to suppress the Republican vote in the state. Cannon later said, "I feared that there would be conflict between the Union men and those who intended to prevent them from voting."[185]

Fisher and Cannon denied asking for Federal troops, but when Cannon met with Secretary of War Stanton, he told the secretary that Democrats and Secessionists were arming at Bridgeville. The Southern sympathizers, Cannon said, were practicing shooting with revolvers, and one bragged about his good aim. According to Cannon, "I had reason to believe they were armed in other parts of the State, and that without a police force there would be very likely a collision between the excited parties."[186]

On the Monday before election day, three steamers sailed up the Nanticoke River and docked at Seaford, where 750 Union soldiers from Maryland and New York regiments, commanded by General John E. Wool, disembarked. These troops were immediately dispatched to polling places in Kent and Sussex Counties.[187] Laban L. Lyons, a special provost marshal for election day, later testified before the legislative committee that investigated the election that when he was in Georgetown, he encountered a crowd of alarmed Republican voters. They told him that a wagon carrying several Republicans had been attacked by Democrats, and two or three men had been badly beaten. The Republicans told Lyons that "they had sent messengers to Washington to see if they could get troops" so that they would be protected when they went to vote.[188]

On election day at Georgetown, voting was held at the courthouse in the office occupied by the sheriff of the county, where voters came up to the east window to cast their ballots. When voters arrived, mounted cavalrymen, armed with sabers, patrolled the courthouse yard near the window where the voting took place. Alfred P. Robinson, a Georgetown attorney, contended that when he approached the window to vote, one of the troopers grabbed him by the left shoulder and told him that he could not go to the window. Robinson told the trooper that he had no business interfering with him and immediately went up to the window and voted. Soon after that, a squad of soldiers was posted near the window.[189]

At Dover, where there were also troops stationed at the polls, there were several reports of soldiers assaulting voters. One voter claimed that several soldiers beat a civilian while shouting, "Kill the damned secessionist!" While the soldiers were stomping the man lying on the ground, the sheriff arrived and called on them to stop, but "several of the solders began cursing him, and threatening to serve him the same manner." At this point, the troops fixed bayonets and cleared the crowd from around the polls.[190]

The Kent County Courthouse in Dover, where voting took place in 1862. *Courtesy of the Delaware Public Archives.*

A few days later, the Union soldiers were recalled from southern Delaware. The Republicans maintained that the presence of the soldiers had prevented hostilities from erupting on election day. Democrats, however, believed that the use of the troops was a blatant attempt to intimidate voters. When the votes were counted, the results were mixed. The Republican Cannon was elected governor by a margin of 111 votes. George Fisher, however, was defeated by Democrat William Temple by 37 votes.[191]

When the Delaware legislature conducted an inquiry of the happenings on election day, Shepherd P. Houston of Lewes, where a company of cavalry occupied the town, was asked, "Did it not seem to be the general impression among person of all parties, judging from their actions, that the troops were there for the benefit of the Republican party, and for the injury of the Democratic party?" The Lewes resident answered, "There can be no doubt, I think, about that being the object."[192]

From the Front: Fredericksburg

I tell you this is a bad war.
—John Carey, First Delaware

During the first year of the war, a Union recruiting station was established in Georgetown, and on September 3, John Cary and a dozen other men enlisted into the ranks of the First Delaware. A week later, John's brother Thomas arrived at the recruiting station to take his place in the Union ranks; eventually, two other Carey brothers, Woolsey Burton and Robert, would become members of the regiment. By the end of September, nearly seventy men had joined with the Carey brothers and answered Lincoln's call for volunteers to preserve the Union.[193]

At the Battle of Antietam, the Cary brothers came out unscathed, and they stayed with the regiment as the Union army slowly followed Lee to Virginia. President Lincoln used the victory at Antietam to issue the Emancipation Proclamation that would take effect on January 1, 1863. When men of the First Delaware heard rumors that Lincoln planned to declare that the slaves in the rebelling areas were free, the news caused a small stir: "Some of the Hotspurs became quite indignant, and indulged in a little intemperate language; but, to the credit of the First Delaware, it can be said that no overt act of insubordination occurred, though some were heard of in other regiments." The men of the First Delaware met and discussed the implications of freeing the slaves and the recruiting of African Americans into the Union army. The First Staters concluded, "[Black soldiers] were as food for rebel bullets as white men, and then contentedly turned their attention to their duties."[194]

As the Union Army of the Potomac (now with General Ambrose Burnside at its head) moved south, the Confederates were entrenched on the high ground known as Marye's Heights overlooking Fredericksburg. Parts of the Confederate lines were protected by a solid stone wall that appeared to make their position impregnable, but Burnside was undeterred. In December 1862, Union artillery shelled the town into ruins, and Northern troops forced their way across the Rappahannock River to occupy Fredericksburg. From the ruins of the town, John Carey, his brothers and other soldiers of the First Delaware looked up at the Confederates on Marye's Heights, which they would soon be ordered to attack.[195]

On the morning of December 13, the men of the First Delaware were roused from their sleep and ordered to be prepared to move with a minute's notice. Around noon, the regiment was ordered to fall in, load their weapons and to to march at the double-quick up a street toward the Rebel position. As they reached the outskirts of Fredericksburg and raced across the base of Marye's Heights, they stopped and turned to face the Rebel position.

A modern photograph of the Confederate position at Marye's Heights. *Photo by Michael Morgan.*

The Delaware troops were deployed as skirmishers; they were to lead the advance line of attack on the hill. From their protected position behind a stone wall, Confederates could clearly see the movements of the Union troops, and they waited confidently for the attack to begin. Despite the daunting task before them, none of the First Staters hesitated since "this was felt to be, in truth, the post of honor, and right nobly did the regiment respond to this call to perform such a perilous duty as to lead the van in an assault of the enemy's stronghold."[196]

While the men were waiting for the order to advance, Chaplain Thomas G. Murphey passed along the line and encouraged the men to trust in God and to do their duty, saying, "Be strong and acquit yourselves as men." Some of the soldiers responded by calling out their last words to be remembered if they fell.[197]

Finally, the order was given to advance, and bent over as if charging through a heavy rain, the men of the First Delaware stepped off toward the enemy lines. Amid a perfect storm of bullets, shot and shell, the Delaware men bravely advanced up Marye's Heights until they were stopped short of the Confederate lines. When the attack stalled, many of the Delaware troops sought shelter behind the bodies of fallen comrades. Despite the appalling casualties, General Burnside continued to order troops to attack Marye's Heights, and the results were the same for other regiments. The ground in front of the hill was littered with dead Union soldiers. In the words of Chaplain Murphey, "Thus, into the night, the battle raged, like the waves of the sea as it rolls in upon the shore, then retires only to come again with unexhausted strength."[198]

One of the last waves of Union troops in the futile attack on Marye's Heights contained the men of the Second Delaware, which was fast earning a reputation for stubbornness in battle. A month after Fredericksburg, the *New York Times* commented that the Second Delaware was "more familiarly known among the veterans of the [Army of the] Potomac as 'the Crazy Delawares.'" The newspaper went on to comment, "This gallant regiment, now reduced to about 250 effective men, fought with a valor and self-sacrificing devotion that won the applause of the whole army…[At Fredericksburg,] it laid its dead nearer the rebel works than any other regiment."[199]

It had been little over a year since the Carey brothers had enlisted at Georgetown, and John Carey had learned the harsh reality of war. He had watched as enemy shot and shell ripped into troops marching shoulder to shoulder in formations better suited to holiday parades than to the battlefield. John's brother Woolsey Burton Carey was among those wounded in the

John Carey of the First Delaware, who became disenchanted with the war and was killed at the Battle of the Wilderness. *Courtesy of the Delaware Public Archives.*

bloody assault on Marye's Heights. His injuries to his side and arm would plague him for the rest of his life. When the news of the senseless losses at Fredericksburg reached Wilmington, Anna Ferris wrote, "Another defeat with frightful loss of life, & nothing gained…Is the tide never to turn?[200] John Carey put it a bit more simply when he wrote to his parents, "I tell you this is a bad war."[201]

Chapter 4

At the Gates of Wilmington

A First for Delaware

One of Dante's excursions into the Shades.
—George Alfred Townsend

Toward the end of December 1861, many men of the First Delaware were sick with fevers and diarrhea, and Surgeon David W. Maull took immediate action. A large stone mansion close to the camp was commandeered and fitted with beds, supplied with medicines and turned into a hospital. During the early months of 1862, the regimental historian reported, "The hospital was soon filled with patients, and although the sick numbered upwards of a hundred, not more than nine members of the regiment died of disease prior to the 1st of May."[202]

If the facilities for treating the sick soldiers were primitive, those for treating the battlefield wounded were medieval. The high number of casualties strained the resources of both armies to remove the wounded from the battlefield. "Ambulances, it may be said," Georgetown native George Alfred Townsend described the removal of the wounded from the battlefield, "are either two-wheeled or four-wheeled. Two-wheeled ambulances are commonly called 'hop, step, and jumps.'"[203] According to Townsend, the sudden jolts were enough to break some of the wounded men's bones. In addition, the four-wheeled ambulances were fitted with shelves where the casualties were so closely packed that they were in danger of being suffocated. After enduring hours bumping over twenty miles of rutted roads, which Townsend likened

George Alfred Townsend earned a national reputation for his vivid reporting during the early part of the war. *Courtesy of the Delaware Public Archives.*

to "one of Dante's excursions into the Shades," the casualties who survived were taken to a makeshift army hospital, where, "in the awful stillness of the dark pines, their screams frightened the hooting owls, and the whirring insects in the leaves and treetops quieted their songs. They heard the gurgle of the rills, and called aloud for water to quench their insatiate thirst."[204]

Those severely wounded soldiers who survived an ambulance ride and a stay in a field hospital and needed further convalescent care were shipped home. But at the start of the war, there was not a single hospital in Delaware. After the Battle of Fredericksburg in late 1862, the lack of proper facilities in Delaware caused Anita Semple (a colleague of reformer Dorothea Dix) to call for better treatment of Delaware's sick and wounded soldiers. The Delaware State Association of the Relief of Sick and Wounded Soldiers was formed, and in early 1863, a swarm of workers converged on Wilmington to construct a facility to care for the state's wounded soldiers. By March, Delaware's first hospital was opened and named for Dr. James Tilton, the first surgeon general of the United States Army. Tilton Hospital took up the block bounded by Ninth, Tenth, West and Tatnall Streets, and it was a compact complex consisting of a three-story brick administration building and six wooden-frame wards constructed of rough planks. The wards were over 150 feet long and ran parallel to one another. Each of the 60-bed wards was connected to a wide, covered corridor that ran along one side of the hospital. The corridor doubled as a common dining room for the wards. Over a dozen windows lighted each ward, and two coal stoves provided heat in the winter. Latrines were in a separate area from the wards, and they were flushed two or three times a day by the Wilmington waterworks.[205] The entire

Tilton Hospital, the first hospital in Delaware. From Thomas Scharf's *History of Delaware*. *Courtesy of the Delaware Public Archives.*

hospital was surrounded by a 12-foot-high picket fence. The hospital took just thirty days to build at a cost of $22,500, opening on March 6, 1863.[206] By August, following the Battle of Gettysburg, Tilton Hospital contained 380 available beds, which were occupied by 95 sick convalescing soldiers and 151 wounded patients.[207]

Wilmington Threatened

People of Wilmington, Arouse! The enemy is upon us.
—Delaware State Journal and Statesman

The Confederate prisoners at Fort Delaware were more restless than usual, and in June 1863, the Union authorities smelled mutiny in the area. The Fifth Delaware Regiment, along with the two militia companies under Captains Lammot du Pont and Hugh Stirling, were relieved of their duty of guarding the Du Pont powder mills, where an accidental explosion on February 25 had killed thirteen men, and dispatched to the fort.[208] Not only did the departure of the militia companies leave the powder mills virtually defenseless, but the troop transfer also slowed production at the mills. Many of the millworkers were members of the militia companies, and some literally dropped their tools and hurried off to Fort Delaware. Mrs. Samuel. F. Du Pont wrote to her husband on June 22, "You can have no idea of the state into which the departure of the 5th Del. has thrown our settlement. The men were hurried off without any time—One who was driving a powder wagon left it en route."[209]

As members of the du Pont family and other Wilmington residents fretted about stripping the troops from the powder works, news arrived that Lee's army had crossed the Potomac and was making its way into central Pennsylvania. Some du Ponts worried about the protection of important papers, and other members of the family planned to "drop bottles of wine into the pond less the marauders should increase their appetite for destruction by drinking it."[210]

The Susquehanna River was only forty miles from Wilmington, and if Rebel cavalry were able to cross the river, they could easily sweep into the Delaware city and wreak havoc in the powder mills and shipyards. Henry du Pont and Governor Cannon suggested to Major General Robert C. Schenck of the Middle Department that two artillery units that were training in New York be transferred to Wilmington to guard the powder works. On June 29, Schenck agreed with the suggestion and passed it along to Henry W. Halleck, general in chief of the Union army, adding, "I am concerned to provide whatever defense I can for Wilmington and the powder works, in case the enemy push any force beyond the Susquehanna."[211]

As orders went out to recall some of the troops from Fort Delaware, a meeting was held to organize the city's defenses, calling for volunteer organizations for home defense. While the citizens of the city were arming, reports reached Wilmington that the Southerners had already captured York and Confederates were threatening the Pennsylvania capital at Harrisburg. From York, which was only a half dozen miles from the Susquehanna, the Rebels were reportedly attempting to cross the river. The Confederates were not a mere cavalry; they were Major General Rhodes's division of infantry, cavalry and artillery. If the Confederates crossed the Susquehanna, the forty miles to Wilmington would be an easy march, and there would be no Federal forces to stop them. Some were fearful that the Confederates would appear on the high ground around the Brandywine at any moment. Ellen du Pont wrote her brother, "Once across the Susquehanna there is nothing on this earth to keep them from riding over all the country between the Chesapeake & Delaware. We have no troops at all here."[212]

On Tuesday, June 30, 1863, the *Delaware State Journal and Statesman* called the people of Wilmington to turn out to defend the city: "To Arms! To Arms! People of Wilmington, Arouse! The enemy is upon us. No time is to be lost. Let us close our shops, our stores, our places of business, and organize for the defense of our State and Country."[213]

According to the *Journal*, the Rebels fired on a Union detachment at Wrightsville, where there was a bridge over the Susquehanna River. The skirmish did not last long, and the Northern troops retreated quickly across the bridge to the east bank of the Susquehanna. To keep the Confederates from following them across the river, the bridge was set on fire and destroyed.[214]

As the Confederates were eliminating the last vestiges of resistance around York, Mayor Vincent C. Gilpin of Wilmington issued a proclamation: "The enemy is on our border. From the latest advices it is evident that he intends to push his forces to Philadelphia, our neighboring city." Gilpin warned that the Confederates would probably cross the Susquehanna and sweep into Delaware. He called for residents of the state to organize militia units to resist the invaders: "I earnestly call upon every one capable of bearing arms to enroll himself in some military company, and upon all those who have any experience or skill in the profession of arms to take the lead in organizing and drilling such volunteers as may be will to serve in this emergency."[215]

As the fighting began at Gettysburg, Governor Cannon issued a proclamation warning that a desperate enemy had invaded Maryland and Pennsylvania. Cannon recognized that the Susquehanna River, with its steep banks, was a formidable defensive position, but there was general fear that the Confederates might swoop in and attack Wilmington. Although the du Ponts had received assurances that the fords of the river were well guarded, Mrs. Joanna Smith du Pont expected to see the Rebels marching down Lancaster Pike at any time. All the family's valuables were packed up, and a hole was dug to bury coins, silver, jewelry and valuable papers.[216] Rumors ranged from the Rebels being at Peach Bottom on the east of the Susquehanna to Southern sympathizers arming the prisoners at Fort Delaware for a massive breakout. Summarizing information from his wife and other members of his family, Admiral du Pont informed a friend, "Our mills are stopped, crops cut & laying in the fields—our gardeners & coachmen gone—our young nephews feed their mothers cows & water the horses &c—two hundred men stepped out of the Powder Mills on the receipt of a telegraphic message…Surely the tables are turned on us."[217] Henry du Pont summed up the situation: "If the Rebels cross the Susquehanna in any force, we shall be burnt out here, we calculate not to leave much to blow up."[218]

From the Front: Gettysburg

The angel of death alone can produce such a field as was presented.
—Brigadier General Alexander Hays

As the people of Wilmington prepared for a possible Confederate invasion, the hundred or so horsemen of the First Delaware Cavalry Battalion rode into Westminster, Maryland, in the late morning of June 28. Under the command of Major Napoleon Knight (whose martial name would prove to be misleading), the First Delaware Cavalry, like so many other First State units, had been relegated to guarding a railroad line. Knight knew that Lee had led his army northward out of Virginia, but Delaware troopers could not find evidence that the Confederates were anywhere near Westminster.[219]

The next day was quiet, and Knight ordered some of the horses to be reshod while he retired to the local tavern for some refreshment. At 3:30 p.m., advanced units of General Jeb Stuart's cavalry division were reported

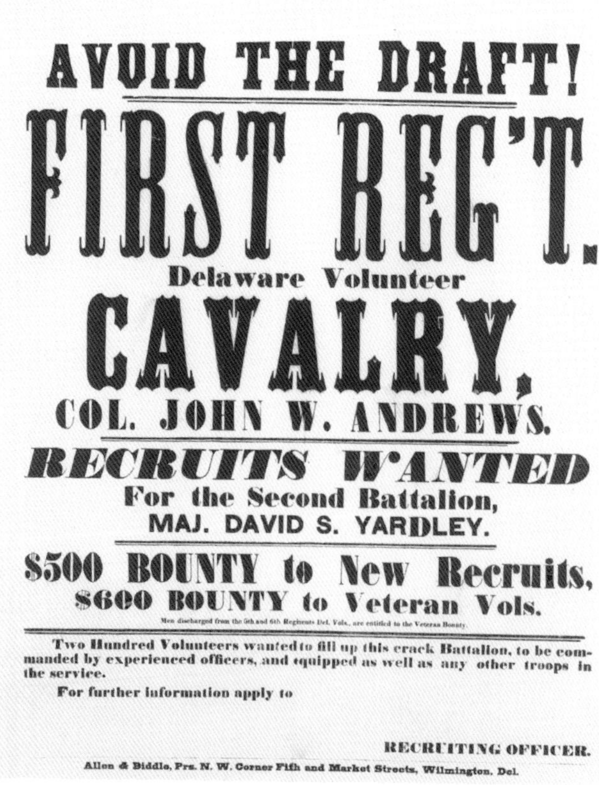

A recruiting poster for the First Delaware Cavalry. *Courtesy of the Delaware Public Archives.*

approaching Westminster. When Knight remained at the tavern, command of the Delaware troopers devolved onto Captain Charles Corbit, a twenty-five-year-old, broad-chested, six-foot-tall man who was every inch a soldier. When he learned of the advancing Rebel horsemen, Corbit ordered his seventy men (the others were on picket and other duties) "to horse" and started down Westminster's main street. Pausing at the tavern to consult with Knight, but receiving no further orders, Corbit advanced at the trot in search of the Confederates. Major Napoleon Knight, on the other hand, slipped quietly out of town.[220]

When Corbit spotted the enemy horsemen advancing into town, he did not know whether the Confederates were an isolated detachment of Stuart's whole division, but the Delaware officer did not hesitate. He shouted, "Draw sabers!" and dashed to the front.[221] The shock of the attack of the Delaware troopers caused the Confederates to retreat, but the Rebels, who greatly outnumbered the Delaware horsemen, regrouped and rode into Westminster again.[222] In the mêlée that followed, Corbit's horse was shot "between the eyes, intended for the master's breast. The charger sank down dead and before his men could close around him the rebels were upon him."[223] After desperate hand-to-hand combat with sabers and pistols, most of the Delaware troops were captured (including Corbit) or killed.[224] The action of the Delaware Cavalry at Westminster helped delay Stuart from reaching Lee's army for a day, and the Confederates were forced to grope their way through southern Pennsylvania. Years later, one of the Delaware cavalrymen was asked if Corbit fought well at Westminster. The soldier answered, "Did he fight well? Why damn it, he was the fight!"[225]

At the same time that the First Delaware Cavalry was fighting in the streets of Westminster, the First Delaware Infantry was making a hard march toward Gettysburg. On June 29, the First Staters, part of Major General Alexander Hays's division, reached Uniontown, about fifteen miles south of Gettysburg. The Delaware troops welcomed the order to break ranks and rest. Most of the soldiers of the other regiments dropped where they halted and were soon asleep, but the industrious men of the First Delaware began scouting for wood. Soon the First Staters' campfires lit, and they blazed well past midnight.[226]

After a day of much-needed rest, the regiment was on the move again, and as they neared Gettysburg in the afternoon, they could hear the cannonading from the fighting. The regiment halted for the night two miles outside of town and, the next morning, moved into the Union line that was forming south of Culp's Hill on Cemetery Ridge.[227]

After they moved into position, the regiment was deployed as skirmishers, and they engaged the Confederates in a brisk fight that lasted several hours.

The Southerners occupied a house and barn owned by the Bliss family, and from their protected position, they were able to fire into the Union line. The Bliss farmstead was about four hundred yards in front of the Federal position, and a detachment of Northern soldiers was dispatched to drive the Confederates from the Bliss buildings. The Yankees succeed in routing the Southerners and, in the process, captured nearly one hundred Rebels. The Federal troops, however, did not occupy the Bliss farm, and later in the day, the Rebels returned and sent a fusillade into the Union lines.[228]

Annoyed by the Confederate fire, General Alexander Hays ordered that the buildings should be retaken and held. The First Delaware and four companies of the Twelfth New Jersey Volunteers were assembled for the mission, and under a steady fire of sharpshooters, they charged on the run to the buildings. The Bliss farm was retaken, and in the process, another batch of Confederates was captured. Four companies of the Twelfth New Jersey, under the command of Captain Richard Thompson, were left to hold the Bliss building. When attacked by a strong body of Southerners, however, they were forced to retire from the house into the barn.[229] Seeing that the Union troops were on the verge of being driven from the entire Bliss farmstead, General Hays, the division commander, exploded in fury and ordered General Thomas A. Smyth, the brigade commander: "Have the men in the barn take that damned white house and hold it all hazards."[230]

Captain J. Parke Postles, who responded to General Smyth's request. *Courtesy of the Delaware Public Archives.*

General Smyth turned to his staff, who were gathered around him hearing what Hayes had ordered, and said, "Gentlemen, you hear, who will take the order?" At that time, Captain J. Parke Postles was sitting on a rock a few feet away, with one arm through his horse's bridle and his head in his hands. Postles had been sick for several days, and he was barely able to continue on duty. When no one answered Smyth's question, Postles raised his head and said, "I will take it, sir." Smyth replied, "Well Postles, you need no instructions from me."[231]

Postles leaped to his feet, threw the reins over his horse's head and jumped into the saddle. He rode slowly down a little lane, passed a little frame building and crossed the Emmistburg Road. On reaching a field beyond the road, Postle urged his horse into a gentle lope. As soon as he crossed the Emmitsburg Road, the Confederates opened fire, which grew hotter and hotter as he drew nearer to them. Postles later recalled, "It was a constant wonder and surprise to me that none of the bullets, which I heard whistling around and so close to me, had hit me."[232]

Postles believed that the reason the Confederate bullets missed him was that he was in motion and on horseback. When he rode up in front of the barn, Postles threw his whole weight on the bridle rein and, at the same time raising both heels, sank his spurs deep into the horse's sides and held them there. The horse, his sides torn up by Postles's spurs, his mouth lacerated and bleeding from the curb-bit, reared, kicked and plunged so that Postles was as bad a mark as though riding at a full gallop.[233]

An officer came to the door of the barn and touched his hat in a salute. Postles shouted General Hays's order, so that the Rebels in the house could also hear it: "Tell the officer in command here, to take the house with one company of sharpshooters and hold it at all hazards."[234]

While this exchange was taking place, the Rebels were firing at Postles from every door and window in the house within sight of him. As soon as the officer in the door of the barn touched his hat again, in token of his receipt of the order, Postles sped away. When the Delaware officer had gotten about three hundred yards away, he began to feel safe, and he turned, took off his cap and shook it at the Confederates in defiance. They immediately gave him a Rebel yell and ceased firing at him. When Postles rode into the Union lines, the troops stood and gave the officer three cheers.[235]

General Winfield Scott Hancock, the corps commander, happened to be riding past while Postles was making his dramatic ride. Hancock stopped to see if the Delaware officer returned safely. When Postles returned to the Union lines, Hancock raised his hat and congratulated the Delaware officer.[236]

After Postles delivered the order to the officer at the barn to take that "damned white house," the Connecticut troops captured the Bliss farmhouse. In the process, they took about forty more prisoners. Postles went over to look at the prisoners, and one of them recognized him and said, "Well sir, I guess your time hain't come yet." Postles asked why, and the Confederate replied, "Well, I had three fair shots at you, and there are plenty more fellows here who had as many." For his actions, Postles was awarded the Medal of Honor.[237]

Farther south on the battlefield, in the vicinity of Devils Den, the Second Delaware Regiment had a sharp fight in which it suffered over seventy casualties. Fortunately, the regiment was deployed to a quiet part of the line and did not see significant action on the next day.[238] On the morning of the final day of the Battle of Gettysburg, the First Delaware remained in place behind the low stone wall on Cemetery Ridge with other Union troops. In the afternoon, an intense artillery duel began, and during the cannonading, Thomas Carey, brother of John Carey, was killed. The Bliss homestead, which had been fought over fiercely the day before, interrupted some of the Federal artillery's line of fire, and the buildings were ordered burned.[239]

Behind the stone wall, the Fourteenth Connecticut, First Delaware and Twelfth New Jersey had collected all the spare muskets, prepared a large supply of cartridges and laid them in rows. Around 4:30 p.m., the artillery barrage ceased, and the Confederates emerged from the woods on Seminary Ridge and moved forward in three lines, led by a strong line of skirmishers. According to General Hays, "Their march was as steady as if impelled by machinery, unbroken by our artillery, which played upon them a storm of missiles."[240]

Thomas Carey, killed by Confederate artillery prior to Pickett's Charge. *Courtesy of the Delaware Public Archives.*

The line of Confederates was an estimated mile long and contained over ten thousand men. An officer in the Twelfth New Jersey was awed by the sight: "The spectacle was magnificent. They advanced in perfect order, the line of skirmishers firing."[241] When the Confederates reached less than one hundred yards in front of the low stone wall, the Union troops stood up and delivered a deadly fire into the Rebels. The Confederate line was staggered as the Delaware troops, "although ordered to crouch close behind the stone wall, most of the men stood up right, as unsheltered as the enemy."[242] The extra muskets were quickly loaded by the men in the back ranks and passed to those in the front, and this enabled the Delaware troops to fire "with regularity and deadly precision."[243]

When the Rebel advance had at last been broken, Color Sergeant John M. Dunn, who carried the American flag, led the Delaware soldiers over the low stone wall. The First Staters, with bayonets fixed, charged into the dwindling ranks of the Confederates, where "a hand-to-hand conflict ensued, in which numberless instances of gallantry occurred."[244] Many of the Southerners "fled from the field, throwing away their arms in their flight. Many threw themselves on the ground to escape our destructive fire, and raised their hands in token of surrender."[245] According to General Hays, "In less time than I can recount it, they were throwing away their arms and appealing most piteously for mercy. The angel of death alone can produce such a field as was presented."[246]

As the prisoners were taken to the rear and the wounded attended to, the regiment was ordered to charge on the ruins of the Bliss barn, which a small group of Confederates had occupied. The Rebels were driven away, and when the Delaware troops returned to the main line, their participation in the Battle of Gettysburg was over.[247]

William Bright Takes a Holiday

Good accommodations, sea breezes, and high living.
—William Bright

On the last day of the Battle of Gettysburg, General Schenck declared martial law throughout the state of Delaware. Although courts and other government bodies were allowed to continue to function, these entities could "in no way interfering with the exercise of the predominant power assumed and asserted by the military authorities." Schenck's declaration stated, "All peaceful citizens are required to remain quietly at their homes and in pursuit of their ordinary avocations, except as they may be possibly subject to call for personal service."[248] In addition, Schenck's declaration of martial law stated, "All seditious language or mischievous practices, tending to the encouragement of rebellion are especially prohibited, and will be promptly made to the subject of observation and treatment. Traitorous and dangerous persons must expect to be dealt with as the public safety may require. 'To save the country is paramount to all other considerations.'"[249]

As Lee led the Confederate army back to Virginia and Delaware regiments returned to Wilmington to guard the Du Pont powder mills, the Union military authorities began to crack down on those they considered "traitorous and dangerous persons." On July 11, Brigadier General Daniel Tyler, commander of the Delaware Department, believed that with the Union victory at Gettysburg and the surrender of Vicksburg on July 4, Southern sentiment was eroding in Delaware. Tyler was downright giddy when he wrote to his superiors from his headquarters in Wilmington: "During the week I have sent two men to Fort Delaware for treasonable language—one of them, William Bright, of Wilmington, a man of some position, and thus making him an example is undoubtedly doing good to the community."[250]

William Bright was a leading businessman in Wilmington who made no secret of his Southern sympathies. Born in Philadelphia in 1814, Bright was trained as a ship carpenter. As a young man, he moved to Wilmington when the town

William Bright, Wilmington developer and Southern sympathizer. From Thomas Scharf's *History of Delaware*. *Courtesy of the Delaware Public Archives.*

was maturing from a small village to a major shipbuilding and manufacturing center. He turned from ship carpentry to home construction and soon became a successful real estate developer. In addition, he started a grocery business, and he also owned the Bee Hive, which was one of Wilmington's largest industrial buildings. At the start of the Civil War, Bright sided with the Confederacy. He believed that President Abraham Lincoln lacked the constitutional authority to force the Southern states to remain in the Union.[251]

For the first two years of the war, Union authorities tolerated Bright's public support for the South. But in 1863, when Lee invaded Pennsylvania and threw Wilmington into a panic, rumors circulated through Wilmington that Bright had written to the Confederates and urged them to attack the city's valuable shipyards, machine shops and powder mills. It was also reported that Bright, a Democrat who had been a candidate for the Delaware state legislature the previous November, had offered to open his extensive industrial holdings to the advancing Confederates. The truth of these rumors has never been substantiated, and it is possible that some of Bright's business rivals instigated these stories in an effort to discredit him.[252]

While the invasion hysteria was at its height, Bright stopped at the home of Mrs. Mary J. Lewis of Wilmington and reaffirmed his feelings for the South. Among other things, he said that the war for the Union was cruel, unjust and unnecessary and that the South had a right to secede and was entitled to its independence. Furthermore, Bright declared that the South could never be conquered.[253]

It is not known who was present when Bright made these assertions, but word got back to the Union authorities, who were itching to silence the Wilmington businessman. Bright was arrested at his home on the evening of July 7 and charged with using treasonable language. After he was arrested, he appeared to be ill and was visited by a doctor. The next morning, however, the allegations were sustained, and Bright was shipped off to Fort Delaware, which, in addition to containing political prisoners, now held several thousand captured Confederate prisoners of war.[254]

Reverend Isaac W.K. Handy, a Presbyterian minister, was also imprisoned in Fort Delaware for expressing sympathy for the South, and he kept an informative journal of his stay there. The crowded casemates where the political prisoners were housed were numbered, and Handy noted that eleven intelligent and well-educated prisoners were in room number one: "In this room is the venerable Col. Waring of Prince George's County, Maryland; and Mr. William Bright of Wilmington, Delaware—both of who are reputed to be men of wealth."[255]

A modern view of the interior of Fort Delaware. *Photo by Michael Morgan.*

Handy immediately took a liking to the Wilmington businessman, who was a member of the Methodist Church. Handy suggested to Bright that he should find something useful to do while he was being held prisoner and proposed that Bright should see what arrangements could be made for a regular prayer meeting. Bright took Handy's suggestion to heart, and the minister noted, "Mr. Bright called in and informed me to commence an evening service. In a few moments, twenty-five or thirty men assembled in No. 7, which is the largest most suitable room for the purpose."[256]

The prisoners at Fort Delaware were given rations of bread, corned beef and coffee. Bright seemed to be particularly humiliated by having to carry his allotment back to his room. The allowance of bread was given out in the afternoon, and the prisoners had to report to the mess hall to pick up their ration, which was to last two days. Bright, who had a number of acquaintances among the militia who were serving as guards at the fort, was embarrassed to walk with his bread, which he wrapped in a handkerchief, through the yard in front of people he knew. When Reverend Handy saw this, he said, "I laughed at him, and told him that I really felt a sort of pride about it and holding my bread before me, took the outside track and returned to quarters."[257]

The conditions at Fort Delaware were so threatening that Bright, who had been ill when he was arrested, decided to take the oath of allegiance that was required for his release. According to Handy, "His sympathies are decidedly with the South; but he is still hoping for reconstruction, and deems it not improper to acknowledge allegiance, so long as his own little State shall continue a party to the compact in the Federal Union. He has been as gay and as happy as a lark since the prospect of his release."[258]

After having spent a month in the crowded confines of Fort Delaware, Bright returned to his real estate interests, and the "happy as a lark" businessman placed a playful advertisement in the *Delaware State Journal and Statesman*:

> *Just arrived from Fort Delaware—The subscriber was arrested and taken out of a sick bed at Midnight on 7th of July last and sent to Fort Delaware, and from the good accommodations, sea breezes, and high living, has been restored to perfect health, and is now prepared to sell or exchange all kinds of real estate to any person that will favor him with a call. Apply to William Bright, Wilmington, Delaware.*[259]

Canteens and Coffins

It appears that numbers of our Southern boys escape every night.
—Reverend Isaac Handy

"My heart sank within me when the ominous name of Fort Delaware was whispered among the men," Sergeant James H. Franklin of the Fourth Alabama Infantry recalled. "I had heard so many fearful tales of this place, told by men who had been prisoners here, that my imagination had shaped it into something that resembled the notorious Black Hole of Calcutta."[260]

When Lee retreated from Gettysburg, Franklin was among the several thousand Confederates who were left behind. On the second day of the battle, the Fourth Alabama Infantry had fought gallantly in a failed attempt to dislodge the Yankees from Little Round Top, and Franklin was among those taken prisoner. After the battle, many of these captured Confederates were shipped by railroad to Fort McHenry at Baltimore. After a brief stay there, several hundred Rebel prisoners were loaded on to a steamer and shipped to Fort Delaware, which had already earned a grisly reputation.

Theoretically, at that stage in the war, captured enemy soldiers should not have expected a prolonged stay in enemy hands. Prisoners of war were exchanged for soldiers of equal rank with the other side, and they were

A model of the barracks buildings outside the walls of Fort Delaware proper. *Photo by Michael Morgan.*

sent home provided that they signed an agreement not to take up arms again until the exchange was completed. In theory, this would lessen the number of POWs who remained in enemy hands. As a practical matter, the sheer number of prisoners involved was a herculean bureaucratic task, and captured soldiers often waited months to be exchanged. In the meantime, they idled the time away in overcrowded prison camps, which harbored myriad problems.

When the first prisoners arrived at Fort Delaware early in the war, they were housed inside the fort. The Union authorities converted the casemates that were intended to hold the fort's cannons into housing for captured Confederate officers and political prisoners. The converted casemates created a room roughly twelve by eighteen feet, with an alcove and a grated window for light. Some of the windows offered a view of the river, and a few presented a tantalizing peek at Delaware City, a small town at the eastern terminus of the Chesapeake and Delaware Canal.[261]

At first, the converted casemates housed political prisoners and officers, but as the number of prisoners of war increased, wood-frame barracks were built inside the fort on the parade ground to hold enlisted men. In the second year of the war, the number of prisoners grew until it was obvious that new quarters were needed to house the prisoners. By April 1863, plans were underway to construct a series of barracks and supporting buildings outside the fort's walls.[262]

Reconstructed barracks buildings. *Photo by Michael Morgan.*

When these buildings were completed, they formed a sprawling network of wooden whitewashed structures several hundred feet long and two dozen feet wide. The construction of these barracks was similar to that of the Tilton Hospital, but there were several serious differences. Inside these buildings, instead of the hospital's neat rows of beds, tiers of open plank bunks lined the long walls. The planks on the three levels of the bunks were slightly slanted toward the center of the room so that while some of the prisoners slept, they slid down until their legs dangled over the edge of the bunks. The prison barracks were heated by several coal stoves in the center passageway between the tiers of bunks. Windows cut into the long walls of the buildings provided light. The wooden floorboards were loose, and the stink of the wet earth beneath the barracks permeated the building. Unlike Tilton Hospital, where the sanitary facilities were just steps away from the wards and flushed by the Wilmington waterworks, the prison privies were located away from the barracks on the river's edge.[263] When some of the first prisoners were led into these barracks, the men began to jump up onto the tiers of bunks, and some of the tiers began to cause the floorboards to sink into the earth, causing a temporary panic.[264] In addition, a hospital, church and other facilities were added to serve the ballooning population on Pea Patch Island that at times equaled

The interior of reconstructed barracks buildings for POWs showing slanted tiers of bunks. *Photo by Michael Morgan.*

the population of Wilmington to become the largest city in Delaware.[265] The island fort was served by a swarm of boats that carried guards, prisoners, provisions, contractors and, despite earlier orders to the contrary, tourists.

A tightly housed population drawn from a wide geographic area proved to be a breeding ground for diseases, particularly smallpox. When the first cases of smallpox developed among the prisoners, they were transferred to other facilities on the mainland. After the influx of captured Confederates as result of the battle of Gettysburg, the number of cases of smallpox and subsequent deaths skyrocketed. A separate hospital was constructed so that the smallpox cases could be quarantined. In addition, the barracks were cleaned and whitewashed, and disinfectants were sprinkled throughout the buildings. The prisoners were ordered out of the barracks every day to get several hours of fresh air. Finally, a vigorous vaccination program against smallpox was instituted. Vaccination had been routine for several decades in the North but not in the South. Consequently, the prison authorities instituted a program to provide vaccine and instruments to the Confederate surgeons so that they could vaccinate all the Southern prisoners.[266] These measures reduced the death rate, which had soared to over ten per day in September and October 1863, to two or three a day.[267]

The measures taken by the Union authorities lessened the threat of disease, but Fort Delaware remained stifling hot in the summer and frigid in the winter. The prison on Pea Patch Island lacked high walls, and the shore of Delaware, home of Southern sympathizers, was tantalizingly close. Dissatisfaction with being held captive and boredom with prison life led prisoners to perform minor acts of rebellion. Instead of making the walk to the privies, prisoners began to urinate near the barracks. When this practice was outlawed, it became "a very common and annoying custom with them to urinate in a tin cup or bucket and throw it out of their windows, creating a very offensive odor about their barracks."[268] Despite being warned against this onerous practice, private John H. Bibb, a Confederate POW, was shot and killed for throwing urine out of the barracks.[269]

In addition to the minor acts of disobedience, the number of prisoners who attempted to escape rose as the general prison population increased. A year before the Battle of Gettysburg, over a dozen POWs appropriated planks that were being used to construct a privy and fashioned two makeshift rafts. On a stormy night, the Confederates made their bid for freedom; one raft was successfully launched. Before the second raft could be moved into the river, the guards arrived, and the prisoners crowded onto the one raft that was floating free from the island and made for shore.[270] Although nineteen prisoners escaped, their numbers were quickly inflated, and reports of a mass escape of two hundred Confederates were circulating through the Union army.[271]

When the number of captured Confederates rose in 1863, Reverend Handy noted in his journal, "It appears that numbers of our Southern boys escape every night." Twenty-seven were reported to have gotten away in one night, and escapes by swimming the river were common.[272] Prisoners routinely collected canteens to use as life preservers. On September 20, 1863, Handy noted that a man had attempted to swim off the island but failed: "He was washed ashore, with several canteens attached to his person. His eyes were eaten out, indicating that he had been drowned several days."[273] Handy was astonished at the number of escapes. He realized that it was impossible to accurately ascertain the number of escapees, but he heard estimates from five hundred to over a thousand. "One thing was certain," Handy wrote in his journal, "many have gone; and they continue to disappear, every week, either singly, or in squads."[274]

Although the escapes were a source of embarrassment for the Union commander of the fort, he sometimes could not help but admire the handiwork of some of the prisoners. Two captured Confederates who were in the prison hospital managed to pilfer building materials from a church that was under construction. Southern sympathizers from the mainland smuggled screws, white lead and other materials to the two prisoners. For several weeks, the two men labored at constructing a boat using the screws as fasteners to avoid alerting the guards by hammering nails. As the boat began to take shape, the pair hid the vessel beneath the floor of the hospital. When the last screw was tightened and the white lead caulked into place, the two men took the boat at night from the hospital and launched into the river. After a trial trip of fifty yards, the Confederates returned to the island to collect what little valuables they had in the hospital. After returning the boat to its hiding place, the men planned to sail their way to freedom on the next night, but someone spotted the two and reported them to the Union guards. The two men, with their boat, were hauled before General Albin F. Schoepf, the fort commander. Schoepf admired the skill with which the boat had been constructed and had it placed in his office. After some good-natured repartee between the general and the boat builders, the Rebels were ordered back to the barracks instead of being returned to the hospital, where they had been feigning sickness.[275]

The flood of escapees, however, caused General Schoepf to take steps to stop the exodus from the fort. All the prisoners were turned out of their barracks, and all the buildings were subjected to a thorough search. The floorboards were taken up, and every hole and corner was examined. As the Union guards moved methodically through the buildings, canteens by the cartload were found, until three thousand of the ersatz life preservers had been collected.[276]

Although using crude boats and floating on life-preserving canteens were some of the most common methods to escape from Fort Delaware, some prisoners used their ingenuity to make their escape. One of the hospitalized prisoners removed a body from a wooden box that served as a coffin. He had one of his friends loosely replace the lid. A burial detail loaded that coffin and several others containing dead Confederates into rowboats and rowed to the New Jersey shore, where a cemetery for the deceased prisoners had been established. In addition to the guards, there were prisoners in the burial detail to do the heavy work. Some, but not all, the prisoners helping with the burials knew that one of the coffins contained a live Confederate.

After the burial detail landed in New Jersey, the coffins were lugged to the burial site, where a long ditch was dug to receive the wooden boxes. As the men were preparing coffins in the ditch, one of the lids popped off, a live Confederate emerged and pandemonium broke out. As the Confederate and some of those who were aware of the planned escape ran through a nearby apple orchard, the guards and the rest of the burial detail scattered in all directions. When they recovered their wits, the resurrected Confederate and a few of the burial detail were nowhere to be seen.[277]

Chapter 5

The War Widens

Rally 'Round the Flag

There is joy in camp tonight over the news.
—Lieutenant Oliver W. Norton

When Lieutenant Oliver W. Norton arrived in Delaware in January 1864, he was a hardened veteran of the Civil War. After Fort Sumter, Norton enlisted in the illustrious Eighty-third Pennsylvania Infantry, which fought in Virginia, Maryland and Pennsylvania. At the Battle of Gettysburg, Norton served as an aide to Colonel Strong Vincent, who commanded the troops on Little Round Top.[278]

In 1863, after President Abraham Lincoln decided to allow the recruitment of African American soldiers and the formation of regiments of United States Colored Troops (USCT), many states with significant African American populations organized USCT regiments; alas, Delaware did not follow along. After the Battle of Gettysburg, Norton was commissioned as a lieutenant officer in the Eighth Regiment United States Colored Troops, which was organized in Pennsylvania and trained at Camp Penn near Philadelphia. Norton was a prolific letter writer; he wrote to his sister on December 10, 1863, "I got here to the camp last Monday and was immediately assigned the command of a full company…We are eight miles from Philadelphia, but the cars pass frequently, and it is not too far for camps, twenty minutes trip."[279]

At the end of December, Norton was dispatched to Delaware on a recruiting mission. His visit coincided with the arrival of the First

Delaware Regiment, which had been discharged and remustered as veterans for three years or for the duration of the war. The regiment arrived in Wilmington on New Year's Day 1864. As the boat carrying the regiment neared the Fourth Street Wharf, a cannon was fired in salute and church bells pealed. After a brief reunion with wives, children and other family members, the regiment formed for a parade to city hall. Accompanied by the Wilmington Cornet Band, a cavalry unit from the Eastern Shore of Maryland, a Delaware artillery battery, convalescents from the Tilton Hospital and a contingent of workers, the First Delaware Regiment marched the city streets cheered by a crowd of onlookers.[280] When the men of the regiment reached the town hall, they were treated to an elegant and bountiful dinner.[281] Norton and the recruiting detail of the Eighth Regiment, USCT, joined the celebration. He wrote to his sister, "New Year's day our whole detachment was feasted in the town hall at the same time with the First Delaware Volunteers, home on furlough. We had good times there."[282]

Before he left for southern Delaware on his recruiting mission, Norton met with Governor Cannon, and they discussed enlisting African Americans into the Union army. In 1863, two residents of southern Delaware had joined the Fifty-fourth Massachusetts Regiment, and Governor Cannon was enthusiastic about the use of black troops. After meeting with the governor,

The Color Guard of the First Delaware with its battle-scarred flags. *Courtesy of the Delaware Public Archives.*

Norton went by train to Seaford, where he set up a temporary recruiting station in a beautiful pine grove that was soon crowded with prospective recruits: "Our camp was thronged with visitors, and darkies who wanted to enlist. There are hundreds of them mostly slaves, here, now, anxiously waiting for the recruiting officer."

The crowd of African Americans burst into song, singing the "Battle Cry of Freedom." The second stanza of this song, which had been written in 1862, obviously resonated with the new recruits of southern Delaware:

We are springing to the call of our brothers gone before,
Shouting the battle cry of freedom.
And we'll fill the vacant ranks with a million freemen more,
Shouting the battle cry of freedom!

Which was followed by the stirring chorus:

The Union forever, hurrah! boys hurrah!
Down with the traitor, up with the star,
While we rally round the flag, boys, rally once again
Shouting the battle cry of freedom![283]

The song made a strong impression on Norton, who commented, "They sing with the heart, and the earnestness they put into the words is startling. Cool as I am I found myself getting excited as I heard their songs this afternoon and saw the electrifying effect on the crowds of slaves."[284] An estimated one thousand African Americans of Delaware, out of a black population of five thousand, slave and free, between the ages of fifteen and fifty joined the Union army.[285]

After a week of enlisting men into the army, Norton received orders to discontinue his recruiting efforts and return to Camp William Penn, where the black troops were based, and prepare to leave for Hilton Head, South Carolina. Norton, who knew what it was to be in battle, had mixed emotions about leaving Delaware: "There is joy in camp tonight over the news. I hardly know whether to like it or not."[286]

FROM THE FRONT: OLUSTEE

They would beg and pray, but it did no good.
—Corporal Henry Shackelford

After Lieutenant Norton returned from his recruiting expedition in southern Delaware, the regiment was shipped to Hilton Head, South Carolina. From there, the Eighth Regiment, including some soldiers from Delaware, was part of a Union force under Brigadier General Truman Seymour that occupied Jacksonville, Florida, in early February 1864. There were high hopes that the Union expedition to northern Florida would cut off the Rebel food supply of beef cattle drawn from the central part of the state, serve as a source for recruits for the Northern army and quickly bring Florida back into the Union as a reconstructed state.[287]

When a reconnaissance expedition indicated that there were few Rebels west of Jacksonville, Seymour decided to march his army of 5,500 troops and sixteen guns westward to Lake City and destroy the Florida Atlantic and Gulf Railroad across the Suwannee River.[288] A march to the Suwannee would take dash, and a fellow officer once said of the Union commander, "Seymour is a devil of a fellow for dash."[289]

On Saturday, February 20, Seymour's sixty-mile dash to the Suwannee River began with a march across flat land sprinkled with thin woods and punctuated by swamps. His force was led by a mounted brigade, followed by artillery and infantry regiments, one of which was the Eighth United States Colored Troops Regiment, which had never experienced enemy fire. Nonetheless, the Eighth was a happy regiment, and the Delaware solders were accompanied by Lion, a large white dog that had joined the regiment during training. A member of the Eighth wrote affectionately about Lion: "He is a soldier, and he has no respect for citizens who may visit the camp and does not hesitate to bite. He attends 'Dress parade,' has musical taste, and shows that he has not been brought up a savage."[290] Full of enthusiasm, the men of the Eighth marched eagerly through the pines and palmettos with Lion at their heels.

Around noon, Seymour halted his army at Sanderson and dispatched the mounted brigade to scout ahead. After they encountered occasional firing from Rebel cavalry, the mounted troops pursued the Confederates for several miles and halted so that the main infantry column could catch up. While they waited, a company went forward to a position where they could see Confederates among the trees in the distance.[291]

While the mounted troops probed the enemy, a battery fired into the trees to determine the size of the Rebel force. At Sanderson, the main body of the Union troops heard the sharp crackle of musket fire, which soon became interspersed with the deep booming sound of cannons. The Union troops resumed the march, and when they reached the advanced units of the Northern army, Seymour deployed skirmishers[292] who encountered Rebel horsemen. Unsure of the extent of the Rebel position, Seymour decided to hurl his entire force against the Rebels, who were Brigadier General Joseph Finegan's army of over 5,400 Confederate soldiers. Like Seymour's Union troops, Finegan's Confederate force had varying degrees of experience, and the two armies were roughly equal. Incensed by the presence of the USCTs in the Union army, some Southerners proclaimed that they would take no black prisoners.[293]

Finegan had selected a position on the Florida Atlantic and Gulf Railroad near the crossroads at Olustee, where his left flank was protected by a large lake known as Ocean Pond. As the Union army marched confidently along the railroad line, the Confederates dug rifle pits and prepared a strong defense position. The battle, which would be known as Olustee or Ocean Pond, would be a stand-up fight between the two armies.

As the Yankee artillery and skirmishers probed the Confederate line, Seymour directed the Eighth USCT to deploy to the Union left.[294] In the meantime, the Union right flank had begun to collapse, and the Eighth was hurried forward. While officers bellowed, "Double quick, march!" the African American troops turned into the woods and ran in the direction of the firing.[295] Lion, the regimental mascot, scampered along with the troops.[296] After a run of a half mile, they reached a position a few hundred yards from the Confederates and took up a position on the left of the Union line.[297]

The Eighth immediately came under what Lieutenant Norton, a veteran of Little Round Top, called "the most destructive fire I ever knew."[298] Some of the stunned and bewildered black troops curled to the ground and huddled in small groups. Others of the Eighth attempted to return fire, but they had so little practice in using their weapons that they did little damage to the Confederates.[299]

Faced with the ineffective fire from the disorganized African American troops, the Confederates pushed forward. But the soldiers of the Eighth regained their fighting spirit and rallied around a battery of artillery. During this confused fighting, the regiment was without an effective commander, and afterward, Norton would bitterly write, "There was no leader. Seymour might better have been in his grave than there."[300]

Fortunately, units to the Union rear that were detailed to protect the supply train could hear the muskets and cannons, and they began to advance toward the sound of the fighting.[301] The arrival of the fresh Union troops stunted the Confederate advance and drove the Confederates from some of the Union guns. Anticipating the retreat, the surgeons had been busy assisting wounded African American troops to the rear. Among the men who were wounded was Shedrick Duker of the Eighth United States Colored Troops, who was hit with a bullet in the left knee. The shot fractured the bones, and the painful wound debilitated Duker, who had to get off the battlefield or be left to the mercy of the Confederates. Dr. Alex P. Heickhold, surgeon of the Eighth, had the wounded black soldiers loaded on to ambulances. He deliberately left wounded white soldiers behind, fearing that the Confederates would slaughter the wounded black soldiers. Heickhold's concern was well founded. Some Confederates made good on their vow to take no black prisoners, and according to one Rebel, "They would beg and pray, but it did no good."[302]

As the Yankees retreated from Olustee, the Confederate officers restored order on the battlefield. The killing of prisoners was stopped, and both black and white Yankees began the dreary trip that would end at Andersonville, Georgia. Duker had begun the bleak retreat to Jacksonville. The inexperienced Eighth USCT had lost 310 men in its confused effort to hold the Union left flank.[303] Among the wounded was the regimental mascot, Lion, who suffered a wound to one of his forelegs.[304] The Confederate victory at Olustee had broken the back of the Union movement in the state. Shedrick Duker spent several months in a Union hospital. After he recovered, he moved to Sussex County, where his nagging wound troubled him for the rest of his life.[305] Duker had survived a Confederate bullet and escaped being executed on the battlefield thanks to Dr. Heickhold's reluctance to leave the wounded African American soldiers to an uncertain fate.

The Immortal Six Hundred

Like cattle are packed in railroad cars.
—J. Ogden Murray

The prisoners at Fort Delaware, as people under confinement everywhere, found ways to pass the time while awaiting their release. Games such as checkers and cards could be fashioned from simple materials. Sometimes, prisoners found serendipitous amusements when the fort's band played in the evening: "Before retiring, the band discoursed some good music; and, during the night, we had a serenade—not intended for us of course; but of which we had the benefit."[306]

Whenever newspapers were procured, they were read and reread to glean the tiniest tidbit of information.[307] Many of the prisoners used their time to manufacture rings and pins from gutta-percha, a natural resin used to make buttons, wagon belts, boot soles and other things. The prisoners used their artistic skills to fashion an endless variety of rings and pins, which were sometimes inlaid with gold and silver and sold to other prisoners at prices from ten cents to a dollar. Among the political prisoners, Reverend Handy noted, "The ring business has received a new impetus, on our floor. An astonishing number of persons are engaged in this work." Handy bought a number of them for his friends and family.[308] Other prisoners, like sailors on long voyages who fashioned ship models, created models of farm equipment. One man built detailed models of plows and cultivators while waiting for his release.[309] Even the arrival of new prisoners became a diversion, with the proverbial cry of "Fresh fish! Fresh fish!" to welcome them.[310]

In 1864, the monotony of prison life was relieved when several hundred prisoners became convinced that they "were going home to Dixie, and I do believe each man had in his heart a resolve that he would never forget Fort Delaware and its cruelty."[311]

Confederate officers were confined within the stone walls of Fort Delaware. *Photo by Michael Morgan.*

After Admiral Du Pont's naval attack failed to capture Charleston, the Union forces continued to bombard the birthplace of the Confederacy. To discourage the Union bombardment, Major General Sam Jones proposed that a group of fifty high-ranking Yankee prisoners be sent to Charleston. In particular, he singled out General Truman Seymour, who, after the Battle of Olustee, had been captured during the fighting in Virginia. Jones asked, "Can you not send me that number, including a general? Seymour would do, and other officers of high rank, to be confined in parts of the city still occupied by citizens, but under the enemy's fire."[312]

The fifty prisoners, including Seymour, were sent to Charleston, and Jones notified the Union forces that they had been placed in "commodious quarters in a part of the city occupied by non-combatants, the majority of whom are women and children." In order that his intentions were not misunderstood, Jones added, "It is proper, however, that I should inform you that it is a part of the city which has been for many months exposed day and night to the fire of your guns."[313]

On June 24, 1864, shortly after the Union prisoners arrived in Charleston, several Union officers went into the officers' barracks at Fort Delaware and called the names of forty-five officers who were to be dispatched to Charleston, "to be placed under the fire of our batteries, with a view of retaliation for like conduct, *said* to have been perpetrated by the Confederate authorities."[314] There followed an exchange of letters filled with invective by both sides accusing each other of misconduct. Cooler minds prevailed for a time, and after the personal intervention of President Lincoln, all officers from both sides were exchanged.[315]

For the prisoners at Fort Delaware, however, the matter did not end there. On August 12, General Schoepf, who seldom visited the prisoners, arrived in time for the morning roll call. He was accompanied by a retinue of assistants, informing some of the captured Confederates that they would be exchanged in a day or two. Some of the prisoners overheard a few of the guards speaking about the release, and when a driver was ordered to prepare his cart to carry bread to the dock, the rumor of the exchange was seemingly confirmed.[316]

On the next day, a sergeant arrived and announced to the captured officers that there would be a roll of names of the persons who would be leaving the fort. Again, General Schoepf, sundry clerks, sergeants and a detail of guards arrived to witness the proceedings. Orders were given for the prisoners to stand on the left of the long walk that ran through the middle of the open area in the fort. First called were several generals. Then the names of captains and lieutenants were bellowed out alphabetically. After the Ms were reached, the names were called out in an irregular manner. Many were overjoyed when their names were called; others were deeply disappointed. Reverend Handy wrote in his journal, "One man said it made him think of the Day of Judgment. It was certainly very solemn, to see the crowds separating, some to the right, and others remaining on the left."[317] Even those officers whose names were not called took heart in the rumor that this was the first step of a general exchange of prisoners.[318]

Despite the appearance of two transport vessels that anchored near the island, a week passed, and none of the prisoners were released, "the names having been twice called, and the rolls fully arranged; but no order comes for the start."[319] All sorts of rumors circulated among the prisoners. Some speculated that Confederate raiders off the Delaware coast made it too dangerous to transport the POWs by sea. Others contended that the Yankees had trouble getting a sufficient number of reliable men to guard the prisoners. In the summer of 1864, an additional six hundred captured Union officers were sent to Charleston, and some of the captured Confederates at Fort Delaware speculated ominously that the authorities at Washington were waiting to see whether the six hundred Yankee prisoners sent to Charleston would be placed in areas exposed to the bombardment.[320]

Finally, on August 20, 1864, the rumor spread that the six hundred POWs would leave Fort Delaware that day. After the Confederate officers were assembled, the long line of prisoners marched to the landing, where they boarded the small steamship *Crescent City*. The hold of the ship had been fitted with a double line of rough pine bunks to hold eight men, four below and four above, where the prisoners were jammed "like cattle are packed in railroad cars." One of the prisoners recalled, "The hold—or hole—of the *Crescent City*, in which we were packed, was below the ship's water line, imperfectly ventilated, poorly lighted, and vile in odor." The guards "were perfectly devoid of feeling, especially so for Confederate soldiers."[321] Although reminiscent of the accommodations aboard a slave ship, the Confederates were not shackled together as the slaves often were.

Four days after leaving Fort Delaware, the *Crescent City* arrived at Morris Island near Charleston. Instead of being exchanged, the Confederate POWs were led ashore and placed into a stockade that had been constructed in front of Battery Wagner, where they were exposed to enemy fire in retaliation for the six hundred Union prisoners who had been placed in areas of Charleston that were being bombarded by Northern guns. After the exchange of the initial fifty prisoners, the Union authorities had stiffened their attitudes toward all prisoner exchanges. General Halleck wrote to General Ulysses S.

Grant, "To exchange their healthy men for ours who are on the brink of the grave from their hellish treatment, of course gives them all the advantage; nevertheless it seems very cruel to leave our men to be slowly but deliberately tortured to death, but I suppose there is no remedy at present."[322]

The Confederate prisoners, who became known as the Immortal Six Hundred, spent nearly two months in the stockade baking under the South Carolina sun and dodging shells from Rebel cannon. After the six hundred Yankee prisoners were relocated from Charleston, the Confederates were moved to Fort Pulaski, where they spent a harsh winter, during which thirteen died of disease. In March, the survivors were sent back to Fort Delaware, where most of them remained until the war was over.

From the Front: Shenandoah Valley

I want you to get out there in the morning and whip that rebel cavalry or get whipped yourself!
—General Philip Sheridan

For General Alfred Thomas Archimedes Torbert of Georgetown, Delaware, the confrontation with General Philip Sheridan may have been the most embarrassing moment in his life. Born in Georgetown in 1833, his father was a bank cashier, farmer and Methodist preacher. Torbert's father was able to secure an appointment for Alfred to attend the Military Academy at West Point, where Colonel Robert E. Lee was superintendent. Torbert graduated in 1855 and began his military career as a lieutenant on the western frontier.

At the start of the Civil War, Torbert was stationed in Utah, and he began the arduous journey to the East. In the days after Fort Sumter, experienced army officers were rare. Some of Torbert's officer friends had decided to join the Confederate army. There were those who believed that because Torbert was from a slave state, he would be sympathetic to joining the Southern cause. Some officers who had decided to cast their lot with the South spoke to Torbert in an effort to convince him to join them. When he returned to the East, Torbert was confronted by Senator Willard Saulsbury, who harbored Southern sympathies. Saulsbury asked Torbert whether he would join the Southern cause, and the army officer answered, "The United States Government has given me my education and I should be a pretty disgraceful pupil if I used it against the country."[323]

General Alfred Torbert learned to "whip or be whipped." *Courtesy of the Delaware Public Archives.*

Despite the fact that Torbert was resolute in his allegiance to the Union, the Confederate government issued him a commission as a lieutenant of artillery in the Confederate army. He became the only documented officer to hold commissions in both armies, but the Confederate commission was never sought nor accepted by Torbert. After his meeting with Senator Saulsbury, Torbert accepted an appointment as colonel of the First New Jersey Regiment. The Georgetown native fought bravely and with distinction for the Union army. Present at both the Battles of Fredericksburg and Gettysburg, he rose in the ranks, and in 1864, Major General Torbert became the cavalry corps commander of three divisions of the Army of the Shenandoah with over ten thousand mounted troopers.[324]

For the first three years of the Civil War, the conflict had been restricted to battles between the opposing armies. As a rule, damage to civilian property was avoided whenever possible. During this time, the Confederate forces had used the Shenandoah Valley as a base to attack the North. Not only did the valley provide a convenient passageway to Union territory, but it also contained rich farmland that kept many Confederate soldiers well fed. In 1864, Sheridan was given the task of controlling the Shenandoah Valley and destroying the Confederate food supply.

For the hard-minded Sheridan, the destruction of the valley's ability to supply food for the Southern forces was simple. Sheridan ordered Torbert to destroy the wheat and hay and to torch all barns, mills and forges that might be useful to the Confederates. Sheridan's scorched-earth policy would eventually destroy the ability of the Shenandoah Valley to serve as a warehouse for the Confederacy, but in the meantime, Sheridan would have serious difficulty with the Confederate forces that still operated there.

During the first three years of the war, the Northern cavalry had been used primarily to protect Union supply lines. General Torbert and other cavalry officers had been taught that defending supply wagons and lines of communication would be more important than engaging the Confederate cavalry in pitched battle. This defensive attitude caused Torbert to keep the cavalry close to the rest of the Union army. He was reluctant to pursue the Confederates on a long chase that would leave the Northern supply lines open to attack.

Sheridan saw things differently. He believed that the best way to stop the raids by the Confederate cavalry was to pursue them relentlessly until they were exhausted or defeated. Sheridan thought that Torbert was spending too much time hovering around the Union supply train, and he felt that the Delaware native lacked aggression whenever he did encounter the Confederate forces.

On October 8, 1864, the two generals met, and Sheridan shouted so loudly that some of the officers outside the room could occasionally hear him. After the war, Sheridan put it this way: "Tired of these annoyances, I concluded to open the enemy's eyes in earnest, so that night I told Torbert I expected him to either give [Confederate cavalry general] Rosser a drubbing next morning or get whipped himself."[325]

The day after the embarrassing confrontation with Sheridan, Torbert attacked the Confederate cavalry, routed the Southerners and chased them across the Shenandoah Valley for over twenty-five miles. Although Alfred Torbert would never be one of Sheridan's favorite officers, Torbert would again never have to be told to whip or be whipped.

OFF THE DELAWARE COAST

This little State, all of whose sympathies were with us, had been ridden over, rough-shod, by the Vandals north of her.
—Captain Raphael Semmes

There had always been a steady stream of vessels sailing past Lewes near the mouth of Delaware Bay, but in 1864, that stream grew into a torrent of ships that lumbered daily by the town. By the third year of the war, the ship traffic began at Philadelphia, where a mixture of steamboats and sailing ships entered the Delaware River bound for the front. At Wilmington, ships carrying gunpowder from the Du Pont mills, textiles, leather goods and other war materiel joined the endless parade of vessels sailing down the bay toward

Lewes. In addition, the ironclads *Saugus*, *Patapsco* and *Napa* from Wilmington's Harland and Hollingsworth shipyard, which became a leading builder of iron vessels, passed Cape Henlopen on their way to subdue the Confederacy.[326]

In 1862, John E. Harmon, a native of Frankford, in southern Delaware, commanded the sailing bark *Wave Crest* as part of the steady stream of vessels that sailed past Cape Henlopen into the Atlantic. There is reason to believe that Harmon harbored Southern sympathies, but when the war began, he took his pet poodle and went to sea in the *Wave Crest*. In the fall of 1862, Harmon stopped in New York, where he took on a cargo of grain and set sail for England.[327]

On October 7, 1862, Harmon encountered Raphael Semmes and the Rebel raider *Alabama*, one of the most powerful Confederate raiders on the high seas. Harmon hove to and waited patiently as a small boat rowed over from the Confederate vessel. After the Southerners climbed aboard the *Wave Crest*, they directed Harmon to fetch the ship's papers. Harmon was then rowed over to the *Alabama*, where he was confronted by Semmes.[328]

The *Wave Crest*'s papers clearly indicated that Harmon's ship had sailed from a Union port and, therefore, was a fair capture. After Semmes ordered his crew to strip the vessel of anything of value, he ordered Harmon's ship destroyed. Harmon pleaded with Semmes to retrieve his pet poodle before the Rebels sunk the *Wave Crest*. Harmon may have argued for special consideration on the grounds that he was from a slave state. Semmes was born in Maryland, and he understood the anguish felt by a native of a slave state that remained loyal to the Union. A few days later, Semmes commented about Delaware in his journal: "This little State, all of whose sympathies were with us, had been ridden over, rough-shod, by the Vandals north of her, as Maryland afterward was, and was arrayed on the side of the enemy. I was obliged, therefore, to treat her as such."[329]

Brushing aside Harmon's plea to save his pet dog, the Confederate commander ordered the crew of the *Alabama* to their guns, and he used the *Wave Crest* for target practice. After Harmon's vessel was riddled with shot, Semmes ordered the bark burned. Whatever sympathies Harmon may have had for the South evaporated when the *Wave Crest* slipped beneath the waves with his little poodle, Dixie, still aboard.[330]

The *Alabama* was far from the Delaware coast when Russell Baker Hobbs joined the ship's crew. Born in Georgetown in 1808, at a young age he was apprenticed to a cabinetmaker. In nineteenth-century Delaware, apprentices worked long, difficult hours in exchange for food, shelter and training. Hobbs could not marry, move away or make any other important decision without his master's approval. Unable to tolerate these demanding conditions, the Georgetown native ran away from his master, slipped aboard a ship and sailed to England. The fugitive apprentice remained abroad until the cabinetmaker died and it became safe for Hobbs to return home.

When the Civil War began, Hobbs aided the Southern forces by shipping supplies through Seaford, down the Nanticoke River and across Chesapeake Bay to Virginia. In 1862, the Federal navy arrested Hobbs, but he was released on the condition that he would cease aiding the Confederacy.

After he was paroled, Hobbs seemed content to spend the rest of the war working on his farm near Milton. A year later, however, Hobbs was notified that he had been drafted by the Union army, and he again fled Delaware by going to sea. A short time later, Hobbs arrived in Capetown, South Africa, where the Confederate raider *Alabama* lay at anchor.[331]

The chance meeting with the dynamic Confederate raider rekindled Hobbs's Southern sympathies, and he enlisted aboard the *Alabama*. In June 1864, the *Alabama* stopped in Cherbourg, France, where the Confederate ship was discovered by the Union warship *Kearsarge*.

On June 19, a crowd of onlookers cheered, "Vivent les Confederates," as the *Alabama* steamed out of Cherbourg to meet the *Kearsarge*. When the two ships were within 1,200 yards of each other, they opened fire. Aboard the *Alabama*, Hobbs felt the shock of the Union shells, which tore large holes in the Confederate raider. After an hour of fighting, the *Alabama* began to sink.[332]

With the Confederate raider settling quickly, Semmes, Hobbs and several other members of the *Alabama*'s crew scrambled into one of the ship's boats. As the men watched from their small boat, the *Alabama* slipped beneath the waves. The British steam yacht *Deerhound* picked up Hobbs and several other Confederates and sped across the channel to England, where the Southerners, including Hobbs, were safe from capture.[333]

On the other side of the Atlantic, the steady traffic around Cape Henlopen continued throughout 1862 and 1863. For the people of Lewes, the passing vessels were a daily reminder of the scale of the war. For Confederate raiders, the endless procession of ships at the mouth of Delaware Bay was a target too tempting to ignore.

In May 1863, Lieutenant Charles W. Read, commanding the Confederate sailing brig *Clarence*, sailed northward toward busy shipping lanes around the Capes of the Delaware. Read had converted the *Clarence* into a commerce raider by mounting a six-pounder howitzer and fashioning from spare spars Quaker guns that looked frighteningly real from a distance.[334] As Read cruised northward, he captured the bark *Windward*, which had left Delaware Bay for New Orleans. In quick succession, Read took a schooner, a brig and the bark *Tacony*, bound for Delaware Bay. Read judged the *Tacony* to be a better vessel than the *Clarence*, and he decided to transfer his command to the *Tacony*. As he was hoisting the howitzer—the only real weapon that he had aboard the *Tacony*—the schooner *Kate Steward*, bound for Delaware Bay, approached the Confederate raider. Read brazenly pointed a Quaker gun at the schooner and demanded the vessel's surrender. The *Kate Steward* meekly complied. Read was now burdened with over fifty prisoners, whom he loaded aboard the *Kate Steward* and dispatched the schooner to Delaware Bay.[335]

In the next few weeks, the enterprising Read captured over a dozen vessels, and the United States Navy scurried to send vessels to sea to capture the "pirate." Read, however, avoided the navy until he sailed into Portland, Maine, where he was apprehended attempting to capture the revenue cutter *Caleb Cushing*.[336]

Read had managed to throw the navy into a tizzy using a sailing bark, a single howitzer and a battery of phony wooden guns. In the summer of 1864, the Confederate raider *Tallahassee*, which had been built in England, slipped out of Wilmington, North Carolina, and sailed northward. The twin-screw, steam-powered *Tallahassee* was fast, not dependent on the wind and carrying a battery of a thirty-two-pounder rifle, a lighter rifle and a brass howitzer. Within a few short weeks, the *Tallahassee* had completed a spectacularly successful cruise along the East Coast, during which it confounded the Northern naval leaders as it captured or destroyed over thirty Union merchant ships.[337]

After returning to Wilmington, the name of the *Tallahassee* was changed to *Olustee*, but many continued to refer to the ship by its former name. On October 29, 1864, the Confederate raider steamed out of North Carolina and again headed up the coast. Near Cape Henlopen, the *Tallahassee* captured and destroyed three schooners and a bark.[338]

News of the attacks of the *Tallahassee* spread and quickly began to mutate. On November 3, W.W. Fulton, an agent for the Associated Press, telegraphed Secretary of the Navy Gideon Welles: "There is a report here that the pirate *Tallahassee* came into Delaware Breakwater today and destroyed several vessels. No confirmation as yet received, but report comes through a pilot arrived tonight."[339]

Welles immediately turned the matter over to the assistant secretary of the navy, Gustavus V. Fox. Alarmed by the prospect of a powerful Confederate warship loose in Delaware Bay, Fox quickly telegraphed Admiral David D. Porter, commander of the North Atlantic Blockading Squadron: "It is reported that the *Tallahassee* has been in Delaware Breakwater today and burned several vessels there. I think it probable that she is looking for coal."[340]

Not wishing a repeat of the *Tacony* fiasco, Porter dispatched several ships to hunt down the *Tallahassee*. On November 4, the *New York Times* used remarkable restraint when it reported the supposed attack on Lewes: "A rumor has been brought here by pilots that the pirate *Tallahassee* came into Delaware Breakwater this morning and destroyed several vessels at anchor there. No confirmation has yet been received, telegraphic communication not extending to Lewes."[341] This was followed by a second dispatch that reported that a Confederate raider had destroyed a pilot boat, a schooner and other vessels. Reportedly, Rebels landed and ransacked Lewes, but there were doubts about the veracity of the dispatch: "The report is not generally credited here, especially as the 4 o'clock Cape May train brings no confirmation of it."[342]

Although the *Tallahassee* had destroyed several vessels near Cape Henlopen, Captain H.W. Ward, the commander of the Confederate raider, had no intention of entering Delaware Bay. Instead, he sailed northward in an effort to find other merchant ships to attack. Eventually, the Confederate raider doubled back past the mouth of the Delaware and continued southward to Wilmington, North Carolina. As Northern warships attempted to locate the *Tallahassee*, the gunboat *Sassacus* was dispatched to the mouth of the Delaware. The next day, the *New York Times* printed a report from Lewes that put the matter to rest: "Persons who left Lewes, Del., yesterday morning, say there can be no truth in the reported robbery of that town."[343]

Election of 1864

I have never been in the habit of making predictions in regard to the war, but I am almost tempted to make one.
—Abraham Lincoln

News that the train carrying President Lincoln would pass through Wilmington arrived in time for the crowds to gather. Despite the fact that there were no plans for the train to stop in Delaware, people turned out en masse to catch a glimpse of the president.[344] When the train chugged by, Lincoln was spotted on the rear platform of one of the cars, and a roar went up from the crowd as the train sped on its way to Philadelphia.[345]

When Lincoln reached the Pennsylvania city, the crowds were equally enthusiastic. The president and his wife rode in a barouche drawn by two gray horses through the Philadelphia streets packed with cheering supporters. Flags and bunting hung beneath the windows of nearly every building, and white streamers each containing the name of a state floated from flagstaffs. Ladies stood at the windows of their homes and waved handkerchiefs. As Lincoln passed by, the president gracefully acknowledged their greetings. At a recruiting station for enlisting United States Colored Troops, two companies of soldiers were drawn up in front of the building, and while a band played "The Star-Spangled Banner," the troops presented arms as Lincoln approached. The enthusiastic troops cheered and cheered for the president, who slowly made his way past the swaying mass of humanity until he reached the entrance to the Great Central Fair. As he entered, the crowd, estimated at fifteen thousand people, pressed down the barriers, overwhelmed the doorkeepers and rushed tumultuously into the building.[346]

The Great Central Fair was staged by the United States Sanitary Commission, a forerunner of the Red Cross. Similar fairs had been held in other cities by the Sanitary Commission as money-raising ventures. The Philadelphia fair was a cooperative effort among the states of Pennsylvania, New Jersey and Delaware. The event resembled a nineteenth-century world's fair, and a series of temporary structures and tents was erected, occupying an entire city block to house the displays that included works of art, antiques, curiosities and other exhibits. When Governor Cannon of Delaware spoke to a large crowd at the fair, he described the results of the work of the many volunteers who assisted the medical personnel: "They speak of a liberality and Christian charity that do honor to our age. They revive the strength and the life of the suffering soldier, and restore him to his county and his family. They give him courage as he goes to battle, and fortitude as he suffers, they furnish him consolation as he sinks, and the promise of a better life as he dies."[347]

The Delaware exhibit featured an art gallery, a display of captured Confederate arms and trophies, a display of antiques and a number of "fancy and useful articles temptingly arrayed for sale."[348] A special feature of the Delaware area was a post office that was operated by "a number of beautiful young ladies, it promises to become very popular."[349] In addition, Delaware offered, at a modest charge, a peep at the interior of Uncle Tom's cabin.[350]

When Lincoln reached the Delaware exhibit, the president was presented with a silver pitcher donated by the residents of the state. At the fair, Lincoln was pressed to say a few words, and feigning surprise, he gave a speech: "My friends, I did not know but that I might be called upon to say a few words before I got away from here, but I did not know it was coming just here." At which the crowd burst into laughter. Lincoln continued, "I have never been in the habit of making predictions in regard to the war, but I am almost tempted to make one." At that his listeners cried, "Do it—do it!"

The president went on to forecast what the future held: "If I were to hazard it, it is this: That Grant is this evening, with General Meade and General Hancock, of Pennsylvania, and the brave officers and soldiers with him, in a position from whence he will never be dislodged until Richmond is taken." At that point, the president was interrupted by loud cheers. When the crowd became quiet, he went on: "I have but one single proposition to put now, and, perhaps, I can best put it in form of an interrogative. If I shall discover that General Grant and the noble officers and men under him can be greatly facilitated in their work by a sudden pouring forward of men and assistance, will you give them to me?" At that the crowd cried, "Yes!" The president concluded, "Then, I say, stand ready, for I am watching for the chance." With that, the audience laughed and then cheered for Lincoln.[351]

The fair showed that the president had some support in Delaware, but one newspaper characterized the contest between "Abraham Lincoln, the ignorant, obscene joker, the tyrant, usurper, the despot as the candidate of the Abolitionists on the one side, and George McClellan, the patriot soldier, Christian gentleman and able defender of individual and state's rights."[352] The election was not as boisterous as the election of 1860. Although there were a number of Northerners who opposed the war (Copperheads), when the votes were counted, Lincoln received over twice as many votes as he had in 1860. The Copperheads were strong in Delaware, which was carried by McClellan by nearly five hundred votes and was one of three states carried by the Democrat.

Copperheads amid Blue Hens and her chicks, an allegory of Delaware Civil War politics. *Courtesy of the Delaware Public Archives.*

Chapter 6

The Fruits of Defeat

Bittersweet Victory

The ignorant representatives of a constituency debased and demoralized by the daunting touch of slavery.
—Delaware State Journal and Statesman

The dark dawn of 1865 found Union troops entrenched around Richmond as the relentless war continued. In Washington, Congress passed the Thirteenth Amendment to the Constitution outlawing slavery, and on February 1, President Lincoln submitted it to the states for ratification. Shortly thereafter, the Delaware General Assembly took up the proposed amendment and promptly declined to ratify it. The pro-Union *Delaware State Journal and Statesman* bemoaned the fact that New Castle County, with a majority of the voters, had only one-third of the membership in each house of the legislature. This enabled the Democrats to dominate the legislature, and they were "the advocates of human bondage, the friends and sympathizers of Jefferson Davis, the aiders and abettors of the Rebellion, the enemies of all progress."[353]

The Democratic majority in the Delaware legislature was based on its support of slavery, and it raised the flag of states' rights. According to the *New York Tribune*, "Almost any, sober reputable Democrat [in Delaware] will now tell you, 'I am opposed to slavery; *but* I believe in letting every state decide for itself.'"[354]

Having blocked the abolition of slavery in Delaware, the Democrats scored an even greater victory when Governor Cannon unexpectedly died on March 1, 1865. The *Delaware State Journal and Statesman* lamented, "By his death the cause of the Union has lost one of the firmest and most able supporters."[355] However, there were no tears shed among the Democrats, who remembered that Cannon had once been a Democrat, and they accorded him the hatred reserved to turncoats. In addition, the Democrats held Cannon responsible for bringing Federal troops to Delaware for the elections during the war. The Delaware constitution did not provide for a lieutenant governor, and the governor's office fell to the presiding officer of the state senate, Gove Saulsbury, one of the three Saulsbury brothers and a confirmed Democrat. The Delaware government was now in the hands of "the ignorant representatives of a constituency debased and demoralized by the daunting touch of slavery."[356] When he was formally inaugurated, Saulsbury declared, "The finger of the Almighty has traced in indelible lines the distinction between the Negro and white races, and any attempt to obliterate that distinction is the result of either blind fanaticism or a wicked and perverse infidelity."[357]

As these events were playing out in Delaware, after months of desultory trench warfare around Richmond and the vital railroad hub, Petersburg, the inevitable collapse came. On Monday morning, April 3, reports reached Wilmington that the Union forces had taken Petersburg, and the citizens took to the streets to celebrate. In the middle of that celebration, a dispatch was received that Richmond, "Gibraltar of the traitors," had been captured. The bells at city hall began to ring, engine houses and worships rang forth a merry peal, cannons were fired, firecrackers exploded, bands played and hundreds of buildings were decorated with flags.

The celebration continued that evening at city hall with a prayer and choir service. An impromptu parade of soldiers, firemen, members of the Fenian Brotherhood, a number of civic societies, the city council and a host of citizens worked its way through the streets of Wilmington, where many houses were brilliantly illuminated in celebration. The festivities concluded with a grand display of fireworks.[358] At Georgetown, in southern Delaware, bells were rung so loudly that they carried over the countryside for miles, and a huge bonfire was burned in the public square in the center of town.[359]

After the fall of Richmond, Lee retreated to Appomattox Courthouse, where he surrendered on the morning of Sunday, April 9. The news reached Wilmington with telegraph speed around ten o'clock that night, igniting another round of bell ringing and cannon firing.[360] On Monday, the celebration continued with the firing of cannons, guns and pistols, firecrackers and loud huzzas. A wagon loaded with bell-ringing Union supporters rode through the streets, and in the afternoon, a crowd made its way to the homes of suspected Southern sympathizers and demanded that they display the American flag. One Confederate sympathizer fired into the crowd and hit a young man in the arm, but when the Southerner was arrested, further trouble was averted.[361]

This unusual multi-column headline proclaimed the capture of General Lee's Confederate army. *From the* Delaware State Journal and Statesman.

For a time, the Civil War in Delaware seemed to have ended as it had begun, with buoyant torchlight parades and high carnival. Even the news of the death of General Thomas Smyth failed to dampen the celebration. Born in Ireland, Smyth emigrated to Wilmington and worked in the city's coach-building industry. At the start of the war, he raised a company for a Pennsylvania regiment and served with such distinction that by April 1865, he had risen to the rank of brigadier general. Smyth was mortally wounded near Farmville, Virginia, on April 6, 1865, and died on the day of Lee's surrender.[362]

In Wilmington, arrangements for an extensive funeral for General Smyth were being finalized when the news of Lincoln's assassination reached Delaware. The *Delaware State Journal and Statesman* announced the news in black-bordered columns, and the victory celebrations were suspended.[363] Most residents of Delaware were shocked by the assassination of Lincoln, but reporter George Alfred Townsend, who had eloquently described the treatment of the wounded early in the war, reacted differently. Townsend, who was in Richmond (where he had covered the fall of the aftermath of the capture of the Confederate capital), immediately went to Washington. Through his newspaper work, the

A. Lincoln.

ABRAHAM LINCOLN

BORN FEBRUARY 12, 1809.

ELECTED PRESIDENT OF THE UNITED STATES, NOV. 6, 1860.

INAUGURATED MARCH 4, 1861.

RE-ELECTED, NOVEMBER 8, 1864.

INAUGURATED MARCH 4, 1865.

ASSASSINATED AT WASHINGTON APRIL 14, 1865.

ORDER!

HEAD-QUARTERS DIS. OF DELAWARE,
And Eastern Shore of Maryland.

GENERAL ORDER, No. 5.

In view of the terrible calamity which has befallen our Country by the Assassination of

President LINCOLN

AND

SECRETARY SEWARD,

All lovers of their Government and Republican institutions, are earnestly requested and enjoined to stand firm and obey the laws and the authorities over them. To this end the preservation of the Public Peace is the first duty of a good Citizen, and the protection of life and property, an obligation we all owe to the community in which we live. It is therefore requested, that all the good people of this District abstain from tumultuous or disorderly assemblies, and from conduct or language tending to a breach of the peace; and should any evil disposed person make use of language or conduct, show any sympathy for the murderers or the horrid crimes just committed, he or they will be instantly arrested and severely punished by the proper authorities.

The General commanding, confidently relies on the Loyal Citizens of the District to aid the Civil and Military Authorities in preserving the peace.

By Command of

BRIGADIER-GENERAL JOHN R. KENLY,

WM. B. NORMAN,

Lieut. & A. A. A. Gen.

Above: The people of Delaware were warned not to show sympathy for those involved in Lincoln's assassination. *Courtesy of the Delaware Public Archives.*

Left: The only known image of President Abraham Lincoln published in Delaware during the Civil War. *From the* Delaware State Journal and Statesman.

Georgetown native had known John Wilkes Booth for several years, and Townsend had seen the actor just a few weeks before the assassination. Using a variety of sources, some of which were unavailable to other reporters, Townsend published a series of articles on Booth and the murder of Lincoln that solidified the Delaware native's reputation as one of America's top investigative reporters.[364]

Lincoln's assassination was largely condemned in all parts of Delaware, whose residents looked forward to an uncertain peace. The political landscape in the First State, however, had changed. Gove Saulsbury was now governor, and the Democrats were firmly entrenched in the Delaware legislature. The state's slaves were free, but the state would adopt many Jim Crow policies that would last into the twentieth century.

A Bright Beginning

The grandest military pageant the civilized world ever witnessed.
—William Seville

Following Lincoln's assassination, the Union forces subdued the last pockets of Confederate resistance, and preparations began for the demobilization of the wartime army. On May 1, the First Delaware began "the last long tramp of the war."[365] The regiment passed through Richmond and Fredericksburg on its way to Washington, D.C. The weather was very warm, and the march was hard on the men, especially the new recruits who had not been hardened by months of marching. According to regimental historian William Seville, some of the men were "becoming exhausted and dying, as it were, almost on the very threshold of their homes."[366] Seville complained bitterly about this unnecessary and fatiguing march: "No plea of economy can justify the measure that resulted in the death of so many of the gallant men who had survived the perils of the battlefield. They should have been transported to their homes by water and rail, as they were carried to the front."[367]

Toward the end of May, the First, Third and Fourth Delaware regiments participated in the Grand Review of the Union troops in Washington, D.C., before President Andrew Johnson, members of Congress, other government officials and thousands of appreciative citizens. The column of troops marching in quick time was so long that it took two days for the review to be completed. The First Delaware Regiment remained in camp near Washington until July, when it took the train for Wilmington, where it was honored by an enthusiastic reception and the regiment was disbanded.[368]

Among the 200,000 troops that participated in the Grand Review, however, there was not a single black soldier from Delaware. The United States Colored Troops were not invited to participate in the review, and the African American troops returned to their Delaware homes with little public fanfare. Slavery would not be abolished in the First State until enough of the other states ratified the Thirteenth Amendment. When this occurred in December 1865, all of Delaware's African American residents were free, but the restrictive laws (some of which were passed in the wake of Nat Turner's rebellion) remained on the books. Black veterans of the Union army returned with their firearms that they had used to put down the rebellion, and a number of those veterans were arrested for possessing firearms.[369]

Those who fought for the Confederacy made their way back to Delaware to an uncertain reception. Washington Vickers, who enlisted in the Confederate army early in the war and was wounded at the Battle of Gettysburg, became a member of the United States Life-Saving Service. Vickers served in stations on the Delaware coast until his retirement in 1915.[370] Russell Hobbs, who was aboard the *Alabama* and escaped to Great Britain when the Confederate raider was sunk, returned to his home in Sussex County, where he was arrested for violating his parole. After a short time, however, the charges were dropped.[371]

William Bright, who had been arrested in Wilmington after the Battle of Gettysburg for harboring Southern sympathizers and had sarcastically referred to his stay in Fort Delaware as being one of "good accommodations, sea breezes, and high living," may have found the political climate in Sussex County more in tune with his pro-Southern sympathies. Shortly after the war, Bright moved to the coast, where he was one of the founders of the Rehoboth Beach Camp Meeting Association. In 1873, Bright built the Bright House, which became one of the resort's leading hotels.[372]

In addition to building his hotel, Bright was one of the leaders in the effort to have a rail line run into Rehoboth, and in 1878, the first trainload of vacationers came chugging into the resort. The completion of the railroad made it easy for residents of Wilmington, Baltimore and other cities to vacation on the Delaware coast, and Rehoboth Beach quickly became a leading ocean resort. Among the many vacationers who flocked to the resort were numerous government workers from Washington, D.C.

Rehoboth Beach was often crowded on the Fourth of July, when many people traveled to the beach to celebrate Independence Day. The crowd of guests who flooded into Bright's hotel during the first week of July, the anniversary of the Battle of Gettysburg, served as a reminder of the growing power of the Federal government. So many government workers eventually maintained summer homes in Bright's new home at Rehoboth Beach that it earned the nickname of the "Nation's Summer Capital."

The Last Battle

The scholars had not been frightened away but were in full force over forty in their old church one [of] *the most interesting schools I have visited.*
—Major General E.M. Gregory

In 1867, three army officers from the Freedmen's Bureau made their way across Cedar Creek Hundred to Slaughter Neck in coastal Sussex County. When they reached the land owned by Charles Schockly, they started down a road that angled through the adjoining land. On the north side of this road, they reached their destination, and the officers stopped to examine the charred remains of the Slaughter Neck schoolhouse.[373]

During the colonial period, there was no public school system in Delaware. The well-to-do planters of Sussex County often hired tutors to teach their children. Less affluent colonists sometimes banded together, building a school and hiring teachers to ensure that their children could read and write. At the beginning of the nineteenth century, a former student wrote that the school was constructed of "pine slabs, notched up, and covered with boards and slabs, a hole cut at the top of the roof at one end to let out the smoke. The fire being made on the ground, with a back of bricks and clay, three or four feet high to keep the fire from burning the house."[374]

In 1829, Judge Willard Hall of the United States District Court of Delaware helped write a public school law that established the principle of general free education for Delaware's children. Hall worked for several decades to turn this principle into action, but at the end of the Civil War, there were only seven schools open to the black residents of Delaware. Following the example of the Delaware colonists, African Americans pooled a variety of resources to build their first schools. After the Civil War, the Freedmen's Bureau was created to ease the transition from slavery to freedom, and the Bureau donated lumber for school construction. Coastal residents contributed labor, land and other resources. Methodist Episcopal churches provided a variety of services, and some of the first classes were held in church buildings.[375]

The bootstrap efforts of the African American residents of southern Delaware to create an educational system were not accepted by some of the white residents of Sussex County. After a school had been completed in Georgetown, a teacher was hired and classes were set to begin. On June 27, 1867, a white mob attacked the boardinghouse where the African American teacher was staying. Although she was able to escape unharmed, the teacher was so badly shaken that she quit her job.[376]

At Slaughter Neck, the trustees of the Methodist Episcopal Church led a drive to establish a school in that community. A lot was rented for five dollars a year, and a frame building was erected. The inside of the new school had been nicely plastered, and as soon as the plaster dried, classes would begin. The school planned to accept students without regard to race or religion.

Before the first class was held, however, several white residents of the area met in a nearby store to discuss the new school. Perhaps emboldened by the apparent success of the Georgetown mob, one of the group in the Slaughter Neck store vowed, "No use to build a nigger school. It shall not stand. It shall be burned down."[377] Shortly afterward, the new school was reduced to ashes.

After the Slaughter Neck school was destroyed, the Freedmen's Bureau dispatched three army officers to Sussex County to investigate the incident. They reported the threats that had been made against the school, but the officers concluded that there was not sufficient evidence to warrant an arrest.[378]

After the first school was destroyed, a second building was erected. While this was being done, classes were held in a nearby church. One of the officers from the Freedmen's Bureau noted, "The scholars had not been frightened away but were in full force over forty in their old church one [of] the most interesting schools I have visited."[379]

The end of slavery did not mean that Sussex County's African Americans enjoyed the rights exercised by their white neighbors. Restrictive laws dating to colonial times and legislation passed as a result of the panic caused by Nat Turner's insurrection were still in effect. In addition, the attempts to guarantee equal protection of the law and the right to vote by the passage of the Fourteenth and Fifteenth Amendments were thwarted in Delaware by violence, intimidation and other means. The right to vote was effectively

The rebuilt Slaughter Neck school. *Courtesy of the Delaware Public Archives.*

denied to African Americans by the institution of a poll tax. Not only was the poll tax a financial burden for many black citizens, but it was also unevenly applied so that African Americans found it nearly impossible to pay. According to the Assessment and Collection Laws of 1873, it was the responsibility of a voter to see that his name was on the assessment lists and that the tax had been paid. Anyone who was delinquent in his taxes would be removed from the tax list (and voting rolls) for one year.[380] Officials could strike names of black citizens from the tax list several months prior to an election and thus deny them the right to vote. The last battle for equality would rage for another century.

Memories and Monuments

Now the fires of Patriotism set all our youthful hearts aglow.
—James Carey

Images of the Civil War began to be engrained on the American mind well before the conflict was concluded. On November 8, 1863, John Hay, one of President Lincoln's private secretaries, noted in his journal, "Went with Mrs. Ames to Gardner's Gallery & were soon joined by Nico[lay] and the Pres[ident]. We had a great many pictures taken."[381] John Nicolay was another one of Lincoln's private secretaries, and Mrs. Sarah Clampitt Ames was a Civil War nurse and artist. Born in Lewes in 1817, Sarah's father was a Delaware Bay and River pilot. When Sarah was still young, her father moved the family to Philadelphia, but she maintained strong ties to Lewes and the coastal region. After the Civil War, her brother, John, became a distinguished member of the Life-Saving Service and served as keeper of the Lewes and Cape Henlopen stations.[382]

Sarah married the portrait artist Joseph Ames, and the couple took an extended trip to Italy, where Sarah studied sculpture and her husband painted a full-length portrait of Pope Pius IX. On their return to America, Sarah was active in the antislavery crusade, and when the Civil War began in 1861, she volunteered as a nurse. Sarah helped establish a hospital in the Capitol building, and at some point, she met President Abraham Lincoln.[383]

It is not clear who precipitated the photographic excursion in November 1863, but it has been suggested that Ames wanted a photograph of the president so that she could do a sculpture of him. She may have also assisted in the posing of several pictures, particularly the image of Lincoln staring

Posters commemorating their Civil War service hung in many veterans' homes. *Courtesy of the Delaware Public Archives.*

directly into the camera.[384] Following Lincoln's assassination, Ames sculpted several busts of him, depicting the president clothed in the toga of the Roman Republic. In 1868, the Federal government purchased a bust of Lincoln for the Capitol; the bust now sits on the third-floor east corridor of the Senate wing. Other copies of the bust are in the Massachusetts Statehouse, in three museums in Massachusetts and in the Woodmere Art

Museum in Philadelphia.[385] In the early years of the twentieth century, sculptor Daniel Chester French used the Gardner photograph as a model for the monumental statue in the Lincoln Memorial. French's sculpture reflects some of the same gaunt and rugged characteristics that the Delawarean, Ames, captured in her bust of the president.[386]

Just as wartime photographs helped solidify the images of Lincoln and other prominent figures in the public's mind, photographs of soldiers were preserved as remembrances of those who served in the conflict. In addition, the Grand Army of the Republic (GAR), a veterans' organization that was formed in 1866, worked to keep alive the memory of those who fought for the Union. Two years later, General John Logan, commander of the GAR, designated May 30 "for the purpose of strewing flowers or otherwise decorating the graves of comrades who died in defense of their country during the late rebellion."[387]

The next year, Wilmington held a citywide ceremony in observance of Decoration Day to place flowers on soldiers' graves in honor of the memory of the nation's dead. The ceremony included "native and foreign, white and black, Catholic and Protestant, orthodox and liberal, all acknowledge the binding force of patriotism and our common humanity."[388] Following a parade, one of the speakers commented, "The day will come when every Union soldier will be prouder of his empty sleeve, his crutches, and his cane, than any other early heritage, and the memory of those who gave up their lives will be dearer year by year."[389]

In the final decades of the nineteenth century, Decoration (later called Memorial) Day was becoming an annual event, and there was a flurry of construction of monuments dedicated to those who served in the Civil War. In Wilmington, stone columns salvaged from the Pennsylvania Bank building in Philadelphia were converted into a memorial for the soldiers and sailors who served in the Civil War. The monument was erected on a small triangular piece of land in the northwest part of the city and dedicated on Decoration Day in 1871. The column is surmounted by a globe and an eagle battling a snake that were cast from surplus brass cannon. [390]

On December 20, 1884, a statue of Admiral Du Pont was unveiled in what became known as Dupont Circle in Washington, D.C. The standing figure of Du Pont holds binoculars in hand as if he were just finishing inspecting a distant object on the sea.[391] In the twentieth century, the Du Pont statue was moved to Rockford Park in Wilmington and replaced by a fountain dedicated to Admiral Du Pont by Daniel Chester French.[392] Outside Delaware, monuments were placed on the battlefields at Antietam

The eagle and snake motif atop the Soldiers and Sailors Monument is reminiscent of the Blue Hens and the Copperheads. *Courtesy of the Delaware Public Archives.*

and Gettysburg to commemorate the service of the Delaware regiments. In 1896, George Alfred Townsend erected a monument to war correspondents, artists and photographers who worked during the Civil War at his private estate in western Maryland.[393] No monuments to African American soldiers have been erected in Delaware, but in many black cemeteries there are isolated graves marked with the insignia of the USCT.

As the generation who lived and fought through the Civil War passed away, the monument fervor subsided until early in the twenty-first century, when several additional monuments were erected. In 2000, a monument dedicated to all Delaware soldiers who fought at Gettysburg was unveiled on the battlefield. In 2007, a white stone monument dedicated to those who fought or gave aid to the Confederate States of America was erected on the

Right: Admiral Du Pont's statue in Wilmington. *Photo by Michael Morgan.*

Below: Monument to the First Delaware at Gettysburg. *Photo by Michael Morgan.*

The tombstone of C.H. Wright of the Twenty-fifth USCT in a cemetery near Lewes. *Photo by Michael Morgan.*

Confederate monument on the grounds of Georgetown Historical Society. *Photo by Michael Morgan.*

Right: Statue of General Torbert near his home in Milford. *Photo by Michael Morgan.*

Below: The *Freedom Watch Soldier* on the grounds of Sunnybrae, Milford. *Photo by Michael Morgan.*

grounds of the Marvel Museum in Georgetown, and a year later, a seven-foot bronze statue of General Alfred T.A. Torbert was unveiled in Milford, a short distance from his house.[394] Also in the Milford area, there is a larger-than-life equestrian statue of a Civil War officer, entitled the *Freedom Watch Soldier*, on the grounds of Sunnybrae, which caters events such as weddings, anniversaries, birthdays, business meetings and fundraisers.

In the early twentieth century, James Rhodes Carey, a native of Sussex County and one of the many Careys who served in the war, reflected on his experience in the conflict. Wounded in the knee at Cold Harbor, the injury was a constant reminder of the war, but Carey kept a positive outlook on his service. Just before he died in 1911, he wrote:

> *Comrades I am sending greetings*
> *After the lapse of long-gone years*
> *Yet life has always held for me*
> *More of smiles than it has of tears*

James Rhodes Carey, who wrote nostalgically about his experience in the Civil War. *Courtesy of Donald E. Carey.*

We were mustered into service
The seventh of March in Sixty-two
And marched away with fife and drums
Dressed in our misfit suits of blue

Now the fires of Patriotism
Set all our youthful hearts aglow
When we gathered at Camp Fisher
Now more than fifty-years ago.[395]

Like Delaware residents who lived through the conflict, time had healed Carey's memory of the horrors of the Civil War. Forgotten also were the issues of taxation, states' rights and slavery, which Senator John M. Clayton had rightly predicted would cause "the storm of civil war [to] howl fearfully through the land, from the Atlantic border to the wildest recesses of the West, covering with desolation every field which has been crowned with verdure by the culture of freemen, and now resounding with the echoes of our happiness and industry."

Notes

Chapter 1

1. Online Library of Liberty, "Speech of Mr. Clayton," oll.libertyfund.org/?option=com_staticxt&staticfile=show.php%3Ftitle=1557&chapter=166720&layout=html&Itemid=27.
2. Comegys, "Memoir of John M. Clayton," 12.
3. Kern, "Election Riots of 1787," 241.
4. Hancock, *Delaware Two Hundred Years Ago*, 25.
5. *Century of Success*, 29.
6. *Poetic Works of Andrew Wilson*, 224.
7. Comegys, "Memoir of John M. Clayton," 14.
8. Online Library of Liberty, "Speech of Mr. Hayne," oll.libertyfund.org/?option=com_staticxt&staticfile=show.php%3Ftitle=1557&chapter=166686&layout=html&Itemid=27.
9. Online Library of Liberty, "Speech of Mr. Webster," oll.libertyfund.org/?option=com_staticxt&staticfile=show.php%3Ftitle=1557&chapter=166687&layout=html&Itemid=27.
10. Online Library of Liberty, "Speech of Mr. Clayton."
11. Ibid.
12. Wire, "Young Senator Clayton," 112.
13. *Delaware Register* 1, no. 4 (May 1838): 318–20.
14. Ibid.
15. Ibid., 319.
16. Ibid., 319–20.
17. Hancock, "William Yates's Letter of 1837," 206.

18. Ibid., 208.
19. Ibid., 212.
20. Ibid., 215.
21. Ibid., 214.
22. Munroe, *History of Delaware*, 209.
23. Hoffecker, "Abraham Lincoln and Delaware," 156.
24. Ibid., 158.
25. Basler, "Speech at Wilmington, Delaware," 475–76.
26. Miller, *Lincoln and His World*, 189.
27. Scharf, *History of Delaware*, 432–33.
28. Still, *Underground Railroad*, 483.
29. Ibid., 495.
30. Ibid., 496.
31. Switala, *Underground Railroad in Delaware*, 26–29.
32. Blockson, *Underground Railroad*, 146.
33. Siebert, *Underground Railroad*, 110.
34. Stowe, *Key to Uncle Tom's Cabin*, 123.
35. Siebert, *Underground Railroad*, 111.
36. Hancock, "Civil War Diaries of Anna M. Ferris," 225.
37. Hancock, *Delaware in the Civil War*, 3, 6.
38. du Pont, *Explosions at the du Pont Powder Mills*, 17.
39. *New York Times*, August 10, 1861.
40. Hancock, *Delaware in the Civil War*, 11–12.
41. Ibid., 12.
42. Ibid., 16–17.
43. Scharf, *History of Delaware*, 1243.
44. Hancock, "Civil War Diaries of Anna M. Ferris," 225.
45. Hancock, *Delaware in the Civil War*, 34–36.
46. Online Library of Liberty, "Speech of Mr. Clayton."

CHAPTER 2

47. David Leip's Atlas of U.S. Presidential Elections, uselectionatlas.org.
48. Avalon Project, "Declaration of the Immediate Causes," avalon.law.yale.edu/19th_century/csa_scarsec.asp.
49. *War of the Rebellion* (hereafter referred to as *OR*), David Clopton to Governor A.B. Moore, January 8, 1861, vol. 127, 33–34.
50. *New York Times*, January 4, 1861.

51. *OR*, Henry Dickson to Governor John J. Pettus, January 5, 1861, vol. 127, 23.
52. *OR*, D.C. Campbell to the Georgia State Convention, March 4, 1861, vol. 127, 122–25.
53. Ibid.
54. Ibid.
55. Ibid.
56. *Delaware State Journal and Statesman* (hereafter referred to as *Journal*), April 16, 1861.
57. Hancock, *Delaware in the Civil War*, 94.
58. Reed, McKay and Wade, *Untying the Political Knot*, 18.
59. *Century of Success*, 111.
60. Reed, McKay and Wade, *Untying the Political Knot*, 18.
61. Ibid., 237.
62. Seville, *History of the First Regiment*, 7–8.
63. Ibid., 11.
64. Ibid., 13.
65. *OR*, Henry du Pont to Secretary of War Simon Cameron, April 19, 1861, vol. 107, 328–29.
66. Ibid.
67. Seville, *History of the First Regiment*, 14.
68. Ibid., 16.
69. Ibid., 16–17.
70. *OR*, Chas. F. Collier to Major General Robert E. Lee, April 26, 1861, vol. 108, 46.
71. Ibid.
72. Ibid.
73. *Official Records of the Union and Confederate Navies* (hereafter referred to *ORN*), Hiram Barney to Salmon Chase, August 9, 1861, vol. 6, 76–77.
74. *Ibid.*
75. "Citizens of Delaware Who Served the Confederacy," www.descv.org/DelawareConfederates.html.
76. Cresson, "Long Neck Steeped in History."
77. Williams, *Slavery and Freedom in Delaware*, 205–6; Harrington, *Reports of Cases*, 288–89; Apostolou and Crumbley, "Tally Stick," 60–62, www.bus.lsu.edu/accounting/faculty/lcrumbley/Tally%20Stick%20Article.pdf; McGregor, "Imaging Systems-Evidence Compliance," 5, www.bcsirma.org/journal/IRMA%20Journal%20Autumn%202002.pdf.
78. Lore, "Life and Character of George P. Fisher," 3–12.

79. *Wilmington Sunday Morning Star*, "One Delaware Legislator Frustrated Lincoln's Hope to End the Civil War," February 9, 1919.
80. Williams, *Slavery and Freedom in Delaware*, 175.
81. Ibid., 175; Hancock, *Delaware in the Civil War*, 119.
82. Williams, *Slavery and Freedom in Delaware*, 175.
83. Lore, "Life and Character of George P. Fisher," 11–13.
84. *OR*, Major General John A. Dix to Secretary of State William Seward, November 20, 1861, vol. 113, 708; *OR*, Memoranda of Various Political Arrest, vol. 115, 312.
85. *OR*, Major General John A. Dix to Brigadier General Henry H. Lockwood, November 11, 1861, vol. 5, 424–25.
86. Gunter, "Journal of My Captivity," 1.
87. Ibid.
88. Ibid., 1–2.
89. Hancock, *Delaware in the Civil War*, 101.
90. Ibid., 100.
91. Ibid., 75.
92. Carter, "Lewes—1791 to the 20th Century," 29–30.
93. Hancock, *Delaware in the Civil War*, 74–75.
94. Ibid., 75.
95. Ibid., 76.
96. *Philadelphia Inquirer*, July 26, 1861, newspaper abstracts, www.newspaperabstracts.com/link.php?action=detail&id=43079.
97. Hancock, "The Devil to Pay," 22.
98. Ibid., 20–21; *Century of Success*, 8.
99. Hancock, "Devil to Pay," 22–23; *Century of Success*, 104–5.
100. Hancock, "Devil to Pay," 22; McPherson, *Battle Cry of Freedom*, 389–91.
101. McPherson, *Battle Cry of Freedom*, 390.
102. Ibid., 30.
103. Ibid., 31–32.
104. Reed, McKay and Wade, *Untying the Political Knot*, 192–94.
105. *ORN*, Flag Officer Samuel F. Du Pont to Secretary of the Navy Gideon Welles, November 6, 1861, vol. 12, 259.
106. Ammen, "Du Pont and the Port Royal Expedition," 674.
107. Maclay, *History of the United States Navy*, 254–55.
108. *ORN*, Flag Officer Samuel F. Du Pont to Secretary of the Navy Gideon Welles, November 6, 1861, vol. 12, 260.
109. *ORN*, Flag Officer Samuel F. Du Pont to Secretary of the Navy Gideon Welles, November 11, 1861, vol. 12, 262.

110. Ibid.
111. Ibid., 263.
112. *ORN*, Flag Officer Samuel F. Du Pont to Secretary of the Navy Gideon Welles, November 8, 1861, vol. 12, 261.
113. Rodgers, "Du Pont's Attack at Charleston," 44.
114. *ORN*, Rear Admiral Samuel F. Du Pont to Secretary of the Navy Gideon Welles, April 8, 1863, vol. 14, 3–4.
115. *ORN*, Rear Admiral Samuel F. Du Pont to Secretary of the Navy Gideon Welles, April 15, 1863, vol. 14, 6.
116. *ORN*, Rear Admiral Samuel F. Du Pont to Secretary of the Navy Gideon Welles, April 8, 1863, vol. 14, 3.
117. Rodgers, "Du Pont's Attack at Charleston," 45.

CHAPTER 3

118. Sprague and Petri, "Eighty Years Ago."
119. Handbill, Historical Society of Delaware.
120. Scharf, *History of Delaware*, 839.
121. Seville, *History of the First Regiment*, 32.
122. Ibid., 32–33; *New York Times*, February 2, 1862.
123. Foote, *Civil War*, 399.
124. Seville, *History of the First Regiment*, 32.
125. Ibid., 33.
126. Sherman, *Chicago Stage*, 212; *Daily Alta California*, June 7, 1852.
127. Sprague and Petri, "Eighty Years Ago."
128. Soley, *Navy in the Civil War*, 59–60.
129. Seville, *History of the First Regiment*, 38.
130. *Ibid.*
131. Morse, *Diary of Gideon Welles*, 63.
132. Seville, *History of the First Regiment*, 39.
133. *Ibid.*
134. Murphey, *Four Years in the War*, 48.
135. Ibid., 48–49.
136. Ibid., 50.
137. Hollyday, "Running the Blockade," 2.
138. Ibid.
139. Ibid.
140. Ibid., 3.

141. Ibid.
142. Ibid.
143. Ibid., 4.
144. Ibid.
145. Blockson, *Underground Railroad*, 145–48.
146. *OR*, Major General Joseph Mansfield to Major General Henry Halleck September 5, 1862, vol. 26, 385.
147. Seville, *History of the First Regiment*, 30.
148. Ibid.
149. Ibid., 31.
150. OR, Major General John Dix to Major General Henry Halleck, September 8, 1862, vol. 26, 387.
151. Reed, McKay and Wade, *Untying the Political Knot*, 83, 90.
152. *Journal*, September 12, 1862.
153. Ibid.
154. Ibid.
155. *OR*, Brigadier General A.S. Williams to Lieutenant Colonel J.H. Taylor, September 29, 1962, vol. 27, 475.
156. Ibid., p. 478.
157. *OR*, Colonel John Andres to Captain Burleigh, September 18, 1862, vol. 27, 337.
158. Seville, *History of the First Regiment*, 48.
159. *OR*, Colonel John Andrews to Brigadier General William French, September 20, 1862, vol. 27, 336.
160. Tanner, "To Save the Stars and Stripes," 83–85.
161. Seville, *History of the First Regiment*, 49.
162. Reed, McKay and Wade, *Untying the Political Knot*, 86
163. Hancock, "Civil War Diaries of Anna M. Ferris," 240.
164. Seville, *History of the First Regiment*, 52.
165. *Journal*, September 30, 1862.
166. *Semi-Centennial Memoir of the Harlan & Hollingsworth Company*, 84–85.
167. Fetzer and Mowday, *Unlikely Allies*, 1–2.
168. Blair and Rivers, *Congressional Globe*, 59.
169. Fetzer and Mowday, *Unlikely Allies*, 18.
170. Ibid., 19.
171. Ibid., 22.
172. Ibid., 25.
173. Wilson, *Delaware in the Civil War*, 1.
174. Ibid., 30.

175. *OR*, Major General R. Patterson to Colonel Lorenzo Thomas, April 24, 1861, vol. 115, 599.
176. Fetzer and Mowday, *Unlikely Allies*, 43.
177. *OR*, Major General John Dix to Major General George McClellan, September 8, 1861, vol. 114, 593.
178. *OR*, Major General John Dix to Captain Augustus A. Gibson, September 8, 1861, vol. 115, 58.
179. Basler, *Collected Works of Abraham Lincoln*, George Fisher to President Abraham Lincoln, August 14, 1862, 379, fn.
180. Hancock, *Delaware in the Civil War*, 115.
181. Ibid., 116; State of Delaware, "William Temple," regulations.delaware.gov/Tour/information/Governors/govs-14.shtml.
182. Hancock, *Delaware in the Civil War*, 115–16.
183. Ibid., 119.
184. Ibid., 118.
185. *Report of the Committee of the General Assembly* (hereafter referred to as *Report on the Election*), "Testimony of William Cannon," 60.
186. Ibid., 66–67.
187. Hancock, *Delaware in the Civil War*, 119.
188. *Report on the Election*, "Testimony of Laban L. Lyon," 113–14.
189. *Report on the Election*, "Testimony of Alfred P. Robinson," 77–78.
190. *Report on the Election*, "Testimony of Charles Brown," 253–54.
191. Hancock, *Delaware in the Civil War*, 119.
192. *Report on the Election*, "Testimony of Shepher P. Houston," 112.
193. *Crossroads to County Seat*, 161–67.
194. Seville, *History of the First Regiment*, 44–45.
195. Ibid., 56.
196. Ibid., 56–57.
197. Murphey, *Four Years in the War*, 89.
198. Ibid., 92.
199. *New York Times*, January 13, 1863.
200. Hancock, "Civil War Diaries of Anna M. Ferris," 242.
201. *Crossroads to County Seat*, 165.

CHAPTER 4

202. Seville, *History of the First Regiment*, 36.
203. Townsend, *Campaigns of a Non-Combatant*, 110.

204. Ibid., 110–11.
205. Smart, *Medical and Surgical History*, 924.
206. Scharf, *History of Delaware*, 361.
207. Ibid., 361–62.
208. Wlkinson, "Brandywine Home Front," Part III, 117.
209. Hancock, "Du Pont Company and the Brandywine Community," cdm15017.contentdm.oclc.org/cdm4/document.php?CISOROOT=/p268001coll23&CISOPTR=3609&REC=12, 150.
210. Ibid., 153.
211. *OR*, Major General Robert Schenk to General-in-Chief Henry Halleck, June 29, 1863, vol. 45, 403.
212. Hancock, "Brandywine Home Front," 153–54.
213. *Journal*, June 30, 1863.
214. Ibid.
215. Ibid., July 3, 1863.
216. Hancock, "Brandywine Home Front," 155–56.
217. Ibid., 156.
218. *Ibid.*
219. Longacre, *Cavalry at Gettysburg*, 157.
220. Wilson, "Captain Charles Corbit's Charge," 157.
221. *Ibid.*
222. Longacre, *Cavalry at Gettysburg*, 158.
223. Wilson, "Captain Charles Corbit's Charge," 29.
224. Longacre, *Cavalry at Gettysburg*, 158.
225. Wilson, "Captain Charles Corbit's Charge," 30.
226. Seville, *History of the First Regiment*, 79–80.
227. Ibid.
228. Ibid., 80–81.
229. *OR*, Colonel Thomas Smyth to Captain George Corts, July 17, 1863, vol. 43, 464-465; Seville, *History of the First Regiment*, 83–84.
230. Postles, "Most Heroic and Hazardous Ride," 228.
231. Ibid., 229.
232. Ibid.
233. Ibid.
234. Ibid.
235. Ibid., 230.
236. Ibid.
237. Ibid.
238. Reed, McKay and Wade, *Untying the Political Knot*, 87–88.

239. *OR*, Brigadier General Alexander Hays to Lieutenant Colonel C.H. Morgan July 8, 1863, vol. 43, 454.
240. Ibid.
241. *OR*, Theodore G. Ellis to William Seville July 6, 1863, vol. 43, 466.
242. Seville, *History of the First Regiment*, 83.
243. Ibid.
244. Ibid.
245. *OR*, Colonel Thomas Smyth to Captain George Corts, July 17, 1863, vol. 43, 465.
246. *OR*, Brigadier General Alexander Hays to Lieutenant Colonel C.H. Morgan, July 8, 1863, vol. 43, 454.
247. *OR*, Report of Lieutenant John Dent, vol. 43, 469.
248. *OR*, Major General Robert Schenck, Proclamation, July 3, 1863, vol. 45, 505.
249. Ibid.
250. *OR*, Brigadier General Daniel Tyler to Colonel Donn Piatt, July 11, 1863, vol. 45, 655.
251. Wilson, *Forgotten Heroes of Delaware*.
252. Ibid.; Reed, McKay and Wade, *Untying the Political Knot*, 252.
253. *Journal*, July 10, 1863.
254. Ibid.
255. Handy, *United States Bonds*, 14.
256. Ibid.
257. Ibid., 17.
258. Ibid., 49.
259. *Journal*, August 14, 1863.
260. Simmons, "Confederate Prisoner's Experience," 2.
261. Handy, *United States Bonds*, 15.
262. Reed, McKay and Wade, *Untying the Political Knot*, 317–18; Fetzer and Mowday, *Unlikely Allies*, 43.
263. *OR*, Lieutenant Colonel William Irving to Captain Ralph Hunt, December 5, 1863, vol. 119, 651–52; *OR*, Colonel William Hoffman to Brigadier General Albin Schoepf March 12, 1864, vol. 119, 1039–40.
264. Simmons, "Confederate Prisoner's Experience," 2–3.
265. Fetzer and Mowday, *Unlikely Allies*, 108.
266. *OR*, Assistant Surgeon H.R. Stilliman to Brigadier General Albin Schoepf, November 6, 1863, vol. 119, 477; Fetzer and Mowday, *Unlikely Allies*, 116–19.
267. Fetzer and Mowday, *Unlikely Allies*, 152–53.

268. *OR*, Brigadier General Albin Schoepf to Brigadier General H.W. Wessels, December 21, 1864, vol. 120, 1252.
269. *OR*, Proceedings of a Court of Inquiry in Accordance to Special Orders No. 443, vol. 120, 1052–55.
270. *OR*, Captain Augustus Gibson to General Lorenzo Thomas, July 16, 1862, vol. 117, 226.
271. Ibid., 225; *OR*, Assistant Adjutant General William D. Whipple to Colonel James Wallace, July 17, 1862, vol.117, 237.
272. Handy, *United States Bonds*, 65.
273. Ibid., 132.
274. Ibid., 160.
275. Ibid., 306–7.
276. Ibid., 468
277. Keen, "Confederate Prisoners of War," 24.

CHAPTER 5

278. Norton, *Army Letters*, 6.
279. Ibid., 192.
280. Wilkinson, "Brandywine Home Front," 301–2.
281. Seville, *History of the First Regiment*, 103.
282. Norton, *Army Letters*, 196.
283. Stevenson, ed., *Poems of American History*, 500.
284. Norton, *Army Letters*, 196.
285. Reed, McKay and Wade, *Untying the Political Knot*, 112.
286. Norton, *Army Letters*, 197.
287. *OR*, Major General Quincy Gilmore to Brigadier General Truman Seymour, February 18, 1864, vol. 65, 285–86; Jones, "Battle of Olustee," 76–77.
288. *OR*, Seymour to Brigadier General J.W. Turner, Chief of Staff, March 25, 1864, vol. 65, 288; *OR*, Seymour to Gilmore, February 17, 1864, vol. 65, 284.
289. Burchard, *One Gallant Rush*, 133.
290. Redkey, *Grand Army of Black Men*, Sergeant Major Rufus Sibb Jones, April 13, 1864, 51.
291. Nutly, *Confederate Florida*, 127.
292. Ibid.
293. Ibid., 210–11.

294. *OR*, Seymour to Turner, March 25, 1864, vol. 65, 289.
295. Norton, *Army Letters*, 198.
296. Redkey, *Grand Army of Black Men*, Jones, April 13, 1864, 51.
297. Norton, *Army Letters*, 198.
298. Ibid., 198-199.
299. Ibid.
300. Norton, *Army Letters*, 199.
301. *OR*, Colonel James Montgomery to Chadwick, March 15, 1864, vol. 53, 24.
302. *Atlanta Intelligencer*, "Corporal Henry Shackelford to his mother, February 20, 1864," March 2, 1864; Letters from Confederate Soldiers, Private James Jordan to Louisa, February 21, 1864.
303. *OR*, Seymour's Report, February 25, 1864, vol. 65, 298.
304. Redkey, *Grand Army of Black Men*, Jones, April 13, 1864, 51.
305. Duker, "Pension Application and Supporting Papers."
306. Handy, *United States Bonds*, 21.
307. Ibid., 35.
308. Ibid., 89, 113.
309. Ibid., 114.
310. Ibid., 85.
311. Murray, *Immortal Six Hundred*, 68.
312. *OR*, Major General Samuel Jones to General Braxton Bragg, June 1, 1864, vol. 120, 185.
313. *OR*, Major General Samuel Jones to Major General J.G. Foster, June 16, 1864, vol. 66, 134.
314. Handy, *United States Bonds*, 454–55.
315. Reed, McKay and Wade, *Untying the Political Knot*, 346.
316. Handy, *United States Bonds*, 503.
317. Ibid., 504–6.
318. Ibid., 504–5.
319. Ibid., 507.
320. Ibid.
321. Murray, *Immortal Six Hundred*, 72–73.
322. *OR*, Major General Henry W. Halleck to Lieutenant General Grant, August 27, 1864, vol. 78, 307.
323. Townsend, "General A.T.A. Torbert Memorial," 13.
324. Biography of Brigadier General Alfred Thomas Torbert, www.civil-war-tribute.com/generate-bio-page.asp?BIONUM=de-07011833-08291880-at-1.

325. Sheridan, *Civil War Memoirs*, 65.
326. Scharf, *History of the Confederate States Navy*, 767; *Semi-Centennial Memoir of the Harlan & Hollingsworth Company*, 268–69.
327. Castrovillo, *History of Frankford.*
328. Ibid.
329. Semmes, *Memoirs of Service Afloat*, 465.
330. Castrovillo, *History of Frankford.*
331. Carter, *History of Sussex County*, 59.
332. Foote, *Civil War*, 383.
333. Scharf, *History of the Confederate States Navy*, 800.
334. Ibid., 794.
335. *ORN*, Report of Lieutenant Charles Read, October 19, 1864, vol. 2, 655–56.
336. Scharf, *History of the Confederate States Navy*, 794.
337. Ibid., 806–7.
338. Ibid., 807.
339. *ORN*, W.W. Fulton to Secretary of the Navy Gideon Wells, November 3, 1864, vol. 3, 314.
340. *ORN*, G.V. Fox, Assistant Secretary of the Navy, to Rear Admiral D.D. Porter, November 3, 1864, vol. 3, 314.
341. *New York Times*, November 4, 1864.
342. Ibid.
343. Ibid., November 5, 1864.
344. Ibid., June 17, 1864.
345. Wilkerson, "Brandywine Home Front," 306.
346. *New York Times*, June 17, 1864.
347. Scharf, *History of Delaware*, 363.
348. Ibid., p. 69.
349. Ibid.
350. Ibid.
351. Nicolay and Hay, "June 16, 1864," 533–34.
352. Hancock, *Delaware in the Civil War*, 147.

CHAPTER 6

353. *Journal*, February 17, 1865
354. Ibid.
355. Ibid., March 2, 1865.

356. Hancock, *Delaware in the Civil War*, 156; *Journal*, February 17, 1865.
357. Hancock, *Delaware in the Civil War*, 165.
358. *Journal*, April 4, 1865.
359. Hancock, *Delaware in the Civil War*, 157.
360. Ibid., 158.
361. *Journal*, April 11, 1865.
362. Reed, McKay and Wade, *Untying the Political Knot*, 142–44.
363. *Journal*, April 18, 1865.
364. Shields, *Gath's Literary Work*, 22–23.
365. Seville, *History of the First Regiment*, 149.
366. Ibid.
367. Ibid., p. 150.
368. Ibid., 151.
369. Hancock, *Delaware in the Civil War*, 166.
370. Citizens of Delaware Who Served the Confederacy, www.descv.org/DelawareConfederates.html.
371. Hancock, *Delaware in the Civil War*, 164.
372. Scharf, *History of Delaware*, 1219.
373. Skelcher, *African American Education in Delaware*, 28.
374. Hancock, "William Morgan's Autobiography," 42.
375. Ibid., 28.
376. Ibid., 30.
377. Ibid., 29.
378. Ibid.
379. Ibid.
380. Munroe, *History of Delaware*, 173–75.
381. Holzer, "Lincoln or Bust," www.historynet.com/lincoln-or-bust.htm; Dennett, *Lincoln and the Civil War*, 177.
382. Stewart, "Sarah Fisher Clampitt Ames," 50–51.
383. Ibid.
384. Library of Congress Shop, "Abraham Lincoln, Facing Front," www.loc.gov/shop/index.php?action=cCatalog.showItem&cid=76&iid=4516&PHPSESSID=595357f14f02a3470802dbdbc33c92e6.
385. Stewart, "Sarah Fisher Clampitt Ames," 50–51.
386. Library of Congress Shop, "Abraham Lincoln, Facing Front."
387. Logan, General Order No. 11, www.usmemorialday.org/order11.html.
388. *National Memorial Day*, 97.
389. Ibid., 100.
390. *New York Times*, June 3, 1871.

391. Ibid., December 21, 1884.
392. Federal Writers' Project, *Delaware*, 300.
393. Shields, Gath's Literary Work, 43.
394. Historical Sculptures, www.historicalsculptures.com/bronze_monuments.html; Delaware Grays, www.descv.org; *Milford Beacon*, "Statue Honoring Milford's General Unveiled," www.milfordbeacon.com/news/x390625369/Statue-honoring-Milford-s-general-unveiled.
395. James Rhodes Carey Papers.

Bibliography

Ammen, Rear Admiral Daniel. "Du Pont and the Port Royal Expedition." In *Battles and Leaders*. Secaucus, NJ: Castle Books, n.d.

Atlanta Intelligencer. "Corporal Henry Shackelford to his mother, February 20, 1864." March 2, 1864.

Basler, Roy P., ed. *Collected Works of Abraham Lincoln*. "Speech at Wilmington, Delaware." Vol. 1. New Brunswick, NJ: Rutgers University Press, 1953.

Blair and Rivers, eds. *The Congressional Globe: The Debates and Proceedings of the First Session of the Twenty-Eight Congress*. Vol. 13, Washington, D.C.: The Globe, 1844.

Blockson, Charles L. *The Underground Railroad*. New York: Berkley Books, 1987.

Burchard, Peter. *One Gallant Rush*. New York: St. Martin's Press, 1965.

Carey, James Rhodes. Papers. Courtesy of Donald E. Carey.

Carter, Dick. *The History of Sussex County*. A special publication of the *Delmarva News* and the *Delaware Coast Press*, 1976.

———. "Lewes—1791 to the 20th Century." In *Lewes, Delaware, 350 Years*. Lewes, DE: Lewes Historical Society, 1981.

Castrovillo, Eugene F. *The History of Frankford, Delaware: 18th and 19th Century*. Dagsboro, DE: Archaeology Excavation, Inc., 1979.

A Century of Success, The History of the E.I. du Pont de Nemours Company. New York: Banker and Investor Magazine Publishing Company, 1912.

Comegys, Joseph P. "Memoir of John M. Clayton." In *Papers of the Historical Society of Delaware*. Vol. 4. Wilmington: Historical Society of Delaware, 1882.

Cresson, Jim. "Long Neck Steeped in History," *Delaware Coast Press*, December 11, 1991.

Crossroads to County Seat. Georgetown, DE: Georgetown Historical Society, 1990.

Daily Alta California 3, no. 158, June 7, 1852.

Delaware Register 1, no. 4, May 1838.

Delaware State Journal and Statesman, April 16, 1861; September 12, 1862; September 30, 1862; June 30, 1863; July 3, 1863; July 10, 1863; August 14, 1863; February 17, 1865; March 2, 1865; April 18, 1865.

Dennett, Tyler, ed. *Lincoln and the Civil War in the Diaries and Letters of John Hay*. New York: Dodd, Mead & Co., 1939.

Duker, Shedrick. "Pension Application and Supporting Papers." Collection of Tim Duker.

du Pont, William Hulbert. *Explosions at the du Pont Powder Mills*. N.p., n.d.

Federal Writers' Project. *Delaware, A Guide to the First State*. New York: Viking Press, 1938.

Fetzer, Dale and Bruce Mowday. *Unlikely Allies: Fort Delaware's Prison Community in the Civil War*. Mechanicsburg, PA: Stackpole Books, 2000.

Foote, Shelby. *The Civil War: A Narrative*. New York: Vintage Books, 1986.

Gunter, Benjamin T. "A Journal of My Captivity." Manuscript photocopy, Fort McHenry National Landmark and Historic Shrine.

Hancock, Harold B. "The Civil War Diaries of Anna M. Ferris." *Delaware History* 9, no. 3 (April 1961).

———. *Delaware in the Civil War*. Reprint, Wilmington: Historical Society of Delaware, 2003.

———. *Delaware Two Hundred Years Ago: 1780–1800*. Wilmington, DE: Middle Atlantic Press, 1987.

———. "The Devil to Pay." *Civil War History* 10, no. 1 (March 1964).

———. "William Morgan's Autobiography and Diary: Life in Sussex County, 1780–1857." *Delaware History* 19, no. 1 (Spring–Summer 1980).

———. "William Yates's Letter of 1837: Slavery, and Colored People in Delaware." *Delaware History* 14, no. 3 (April 1971).

Handbill for Hopkinson Hall, Historical Society of Delaware.

Handy, Isaac W.K. *United States Bonds; or Duress by Federal Authority*. Baltimore: Turnbull Brothers, 1874.

Harrington, Samuel. *Reports of Cases Argued and Adjudged in the Superior Court and Court of Errors and Appeal*. Vol. 2. Dover, DE: S. Kimmey, 1841.

Hoffecker, Carol E. "Abraham Lincoln and Delaware." *Delaware History* 32, no. 3 (Fall–Winter 2008).

Hollyday, Frederic B.M. "Running the Blockade: Henry Hollyday Joins the Confederacy." *Maryland Historical Magazine* 41, no. 1 (March 1946).

Jones, Major-General Samuel, CSA. "The Battle of Olustee, or Ocean Pond, Florida." In *Battles and Leaders*. Vol. 4. Secaucus, NJ: Castle Books, n.d.

Keen, Nancy Travis. "Confederate Prisoners of War at Fort Delaware." *Delaware History* 13, no. 1 (April 1968).

Kern, John R. "The Election Riots of 1787 in Sussex County, Delaware." *Delaware History* 22, no. 4 (Fall–Winter 1987).

Letters from Confederate Soldiers. United Daughters of the Confederacy Collection, Georgia State Archives. Private James Jordan to Louisa, February 21, 1864.

Longacre, Edward G. *The Cavalry at Gettysburg*. Lincoln: University of Nebraska Press, 1993.

Lore, Charles B. "The Life and Character of George P. Fisher." *Papers of the Historical Society of Delaware*, 3–12. Wilmington: Historical Society of Delaware, 1902.

Maclay, Edgar Stanton. *A History of the United States Navy*. Vol. 2. New York: D. Appleton and Company, 1894.

McPherson, James. *Battle Cry of Freedom*. New York: Oxford University Press, 1988.

Miller, Richard Lawrence. *Lincoln and His World. Volume 3, The Rise to National Prominence, 1843–1853*. Jefferson, NC: McFarland & Company, 2011.

Morse, John T. *Diary of Gideon Welles*. Vol. 1. New York: Houghton Mifflin Company, 1911.

Munroe, John A. *History of Delaware*. Newark: University of Delaware Press, 1979.

Murphey, Thomas G. *Four Years in the War*. Philadelphia: James S. Claxton, 1866.

Murray, J. Ogden. *The Immortal Six Hundred: A Story of Cruelty to Confederate Prisoners of War*. Roanoke, VA: Stone Printing and Manufacturing Co., 1911.

The National Memorial Day: A Record of the Ceremonies. Washington, D.C.: Headquarters Grand Army of the Republic, 1870.

New York Times, January 4, 1861; February. 2, 1862; January 13, 1863; November 4, 1864; November 5, 1864; June 17, 1864; June 3, 1871; December 21, 1884.

Nicolay, John G., and John Hay, eds. "June 16, 1864.—Speech at a Sanitary Fair in Philadelphia, Pennsylvania." In *Abraham Lincoln, Complete Works*. Vol. 2. New York: Century Co., 1907.

Norton, Oliver W. *Army Letters*. Chicago: O.I. Deming, printer, 1903.

Nutly, William H. *Confederate Florida: The Road to Olustee*. Tuscaloosa,: University of Alabama Press, 1990.

Official Records of the Union and Confederate Navies during the War of the Rebellion. Washington, D.C.: U.S. Government Printing Office, 1897–1917.

The Poetic Works of Andrew Wilson. Belfast: John Henderson, n.d.

Postles, Captain J. Parks. "A Most Heroic and Hazardous Ride at Gettysburg." In *Deeds of Valor*, edited by W.F. Beyer and O.F. Keydel. Stamford, CT: Longmeadow Press, 1994.

Redkey, Edwin S., ed. *A Grand Army of Black Men: Letters from African-American Soldiers in the Union Army, 1861–1865*. New York: Press Syndicate of the University of Cambridge, 1993.

Reed, Thomas J.W., Andrew McKay and Rev. Anthony R. Wade. *Untying the Political Knot: Delaware During the War Between the States.* Wilmington, NC: Broadfoot Publishing Company, 2001.

Report of the Committee of the General Assembly of the State of Delaware in Regard to the Interference of the United States Troops with the General Election. Dover, DE: James Kirk, 1863.

Rodgers, Rear Admiral C.R.P. "Du Pont's Attack at Charleston." *Battles and Leaders*. Vol. 4. Reprint, Secaucus, NJ: Castle Books, n.d.

Scharf, J. Thomas. *History of the Confederate States Navy*. Reprint, New York: Gramercy Books, 1996.

———. *History of Delaware*. Vol. 1. Philadelphia: L.J. Richards and Co., 1888.

Semi-Centennial Memoir of the Harlan & Hollingsworth Company. Wilmington, DE, 1886.

Semmes, Raphael. *Memoirs of Service Afloat During the War Between the States.* Baltimore: Kelley, Piet & Co., 1869.

Seville, William. *History of the First Regiment, Delaware Volunteers*. Wilmington, DE, 1884. Reprint, Baltimore: Longstreet House, 1986.

Sheridan, Philip. *Civil War Memoirs*. New York: Bantam Books, 1991.

Sherman, Robert L. *Chicago Stage, Its Records and Achievements*. Vol. 1. Chicago: self-published, 1947.

Shields, Jerry. *Gath's Literary Work and Folk and Other Selected Writings of George Alfred Townsend*. Wilmington: Delaware Heritage Press, 1996.

Siebert, Wilbur H. *The Underground Railroad from Slavery to Freedom*. New York: Macmillan Company, 1899.

Simmons, R. Hugh. "A Confederate Prisoner's Experience in the New Barracks." *Fort Delaware Notes* 52 (February 2002).

Skelcher, Bradley. *African American Education in Delaware: A History through Photographs, 1865–1930*. Wilmington: Delaware Heritage Press, 1999.

Smart, Major Charles. *Medical and Surgical History of the War of the Rebellion*. Part 3, Vol. 1. Washington, D.C.: Government Printing Office, 1888.

Soley, James Russell. *The Navy in the Civil War. Vol. 1, Blockade and Cruisers*. New York: Charles Scribner's Sons, 1885.

Sprague, C., lyricist, J.F. Petri, music. "Eighty Years Ago." J.F. Petri Publication. New York: William Hall & Son, 1856.

Stevenson, Burton Egbert, ed. *Poems of American History*. Boston: Houghton Mifflin Company, 1992.

Stewart, Robert G. "Sarah Fisher Clampitt Ames." *Journal of the Lewes Historical Society* 7 (November 2004): 50–51.

Still, William. *The Underground Railroad.* Philadelphia: William Still, 1886.

Stowe, Harriet Beecher. *A Key to Uncle Tom's Cabin*. London: Sampson Low, Son and Company, 1853.

Switala, William J. *Underground Railroad in Delaware, Maryland, and West Virginia*. Mechanicsburg, PA: Stackpole Books, 2004.

Tanner, Charles. "To Save the Stars and Stripes." In *Deeds of Valor*, 83–85. Stamford, CT: Longmeadow Press, 1994.

Townsend, George Alfred. *Campaigns of a Non-Combatant*. New York: Blelock and Company, 1866.

———. "General T.A. Torbert Memorial." In *Historical and Biographical Papers*. Wilmington: Historical Society of Delaware, 1922.

War of the Rebellion: A Compilation of the Official Records of the Union and Confederate Armies. Washington, D.C.: U.S. Government Printing Office, 1880–1901.

Weddle, Kevin. *Lincoln's Tragic Admiral: The Life of Samuel Francis Du Pont.* Charlottesville: University of Virginia Press, 2005.

Wilkinson, Norman B. "The Brandywine Home Front During the Civil War, Parts I–IV: 1864–1865." *Delaware History*. Part I, 9, no. 3 (April 1961); part II, 10, no. 3 (April 1963); part III, 11, no. 2 (October 1964); part IV, 11, no. 4 (October 1965).

Williams, William H. *Slavery and Freedom in Delaware, 1639–1865*. Wilmington, DE: Scholarly Resources Inc., 1996.

Wilmington Sunday Morning Star, February 9, 1919.

Wilson, James H. "Captain Charles Corbit's Charge at Westminster." *Papers of the Historical Society of Delaware.* No. 62. Wilmington: Historical Society of Delaware, 1913.

Wilson, W. Emerson. *Delaware in the Civil War.* N.p.: Fort Delaware Society, n.d.

———. *Forgotten Heroes of Delaware*. Cambridge, MA: Deltos Publishing Company, 1969.

Wire, Richard Arden. "Young Senator Clayton and the Early Jackson Years." *Delaware History* 18, No. 2 (Fall–Winter 1976).

ONLINE SOURCES

Apostolou, Nicolas, and D. Larry Crumbley. "The Tally Stick: The First Internal Control?" *ACFEI News*, 60–62. www.bus.lsu.edu/accounting/faculty/lcrumbley/Tally%20Stick%20Article.pdf.

The Avalon Project, Documents in Law, History and Diplomacy. "Declaration of the Immediate Causes Which Induce and Justify the Secession of South Carolina from the Federal Union." avalon.law.yale.edu/19th_century/csa_scarsec.asp.

Biography of Brigadier General Alfred Thomas Torbert. www.civil-war-tribute.com/generate-bio-page.asp?BIONUM=de-07011833-08291880-at-1.

Citizens of Delaware Who Served the Confederacy. www.descv.org/DelawareConfederates.html.

David Leip's Atlas of U. S. Presidential Elections. uselectionatlas.org.

The Delaware Grays, Sons of Confederate Veterans Camp #2068. www.descv.org.

Hancock, Harold B. "The Du Pont Company and the Brandywine Community during the Civil War." cdm15017.contentdm.oclc.org/cdm4/document.php?CISOROOT=/p268001coll23&CISOPTR=3609&REC=12.

Historical Sculptures. www.historicalsculptures.com/bronze_monuments.html.

Holzer, Harold. "Lincoln or Bust." HistoryNet.com. August 18, 2009. www.historynet.com/lincoln-or-bust.htm.

Library of Congress Shop. "Abraham Lincoln, Facing Front." www.loc.gov/shop/index.php?action=cCatalog.showItem&cid=76&iid=4516&PHPSESSID=595357f14f02a3470802dbdbc33c92e6.

Logan, General John. "General Order No. 11, May 5, 1868." www.usmemorialday.org/order11.html.

McGregor, Fiona. "Imaging Systems-Evidence Compliance." *IRMA Journal* 13, no. 2 (Autumn 2002). www.bcsirma.org/journal/IRMA%20Journal%20Autumn%202002.pdf.

Milford Beacon. "Statue Honoring Milford's General Unveiled." July 4, 2008. www.milfordbeacon.com/news/x390625369/Statue-honoring-Milford-s-general-unveiled.

Online Library of Liberty. "Speech of Mr. Hayne, of South Carolina, January 25, 1830"; "Speech of Mr. Webster, of Massachusetts, January 26 and 27, 1830"; and "Speech of Mr. Clayton, of Delaware, March 4, 1830." oll.libertyfund.org/?option=com_staticxt&staticfile=show.php%3Ftitle=1557&chapter=166720&layout=html&Itemid=27.

Philadelphia Inquirer, July 26, 1861. Newspaper abstracts. www.newspaperabstracts.com/link.php?action=detail&id=43079.

State of Delaware. "William Temple." regulations.delaware.gov/Tour/information/Governors/govs-14.shtml.

Index

D

E

F

N

O

P

R

S

About the Author

Photo by Madelyn Morgan.

Michael Morgan has been writing freelance newspaper articles on the history of coastal Delaware for over three decades. He is the author of the "Delaware Diary," which appears weekly in the *Delaware Coast Press*, and the "Sussex Journal," which is a weekly feature of the *Wave*. Morgan has also published articles in the *Civil War Times*, *America's Civil War*, the *Baltimore Sun*, *Maryland Magazine*, *Chesapeake Bay Magazine*, *World War II Magazine* and other national publications. Morgan's look at history is marked by a lively, storytelling style that has made his writing and lectures popular. Michael Morgan is also the author of *Pirates and Patriots: Tales of the Delaware Coast*, *Rehoboth Beach: A History of Surf and Sand*, *Bethany Beach: A Brief History* and *Ocean City: Going Down the Ocean*.